SYRACUSE UNIVERSITY 15608026
Education and state politics;
LB 2805.U5

Education and State Politics

Education and State Politics

Michael D. USDAN

David W. MINAR

Emanuel HURWITZ, Jr.

The Developing Relationship Between Elementary-Secondary and Higher Education

Teachers College Press
Teachers College, Columbia University

© 1969 by Teachers College, Columbia University

Library of Congress Catalog Card Number: 69-17673

Manufactured in the United States of America

Preface

This study was conceived out of concern for American educational policy and interest in the intricacies of the politics of education. Its focus falls on an important but little discussed fact of life, the sharp division in our society between elementary and secondary education on the one hand and higher education on the other. We are convinced that this separation has profound implications for educational decision-making for the future.

Our efforts have been directed to describing in a comparative way the political relationships between the two levels in a dozen states, with particular attention to the forces of change. Limited resources have prohibited as much depth of investigation as would be ideal. This report should, therefore, be seen as a pilot study, a preliminary attempt at analysis of a subject that deserves much more attention. We hope it may be of interest to policy-makers, and to students of educational organization and state political systems alike.

The report is composed of three chapters and a concluding statement. Chapter I describes the problem under investigation and outlines the design of the study. Chapter II is a summary of the twelve detailed individual state reports which were prepared for the sponsors of the project, the Education Commission of the United States and the American Council on Education. Emphasis has been focused in these profiles on a description of the educational decision-making systems in each state and on the issues affecting interlevel relationships.

Chapter III, which is an analysis of the major elements in interlevel educational relationships, draws upon the profiles in Chapter II for its generalizations. The analysis represents an effort to compare the relationships in the various states by using the concepts of conflict and cooperation as a basic framework.

The concluding statement is a summary of the entire study. It emphasizes the trends and directions for educational decision-making suggested by the analysis in Chapter III and also warns of consequential implications if action is not soon taken on the lack of overall coordination in determining educational policy.

We are indebted to a great number of people for making this report possible. Particular thanks are due to the Education Commission of the States and the American Council on Education for funding this project. Neither sponsoring organization bears any responsibility for this report. The authors alone are responsible for its contents.

A special debt of gratitude is owed to Professor Robert O. Berdahl, Director of the American Council on Education's Study of Statewide Systems of Higher Education. Professor Berdahl was instrumental in the initiation and implementation of this effort. He obtained the necessary financial support for us to carry out the endeavor and along with Miss Jane Graham of the Staff of the American Council on Education provided indispensable assistance throughout the course of the study.

We are also particularly indebted to Dr. Kenneth H. Hansen, director of Program Development for the Education Commission of the States, for his thoughtful cooperation and assistance.

We should also take this opportunity to express our sincere appreciation to the dozens of educators, officials of government and private organizations, and other concerned citizens who generously granted us interview time during our visits to the twelve states discussed in the subsequent pages.

Michael D. Usdan
David W. Minar
Emanuel Hurwitz, Jr.

New York, New York
June 12, 1968

Foreword

Two myths—comfortable but inaccurate—have stood in the way of our understanding of how the American educational system actually operates at the state level.

One is the belief that education and politics do not mix: let's keep politics out of education, we say, and education out of politics.

The other equally misleading myth is that there are two inherently distinct and separate kinds of education: the "common schools," elementary and secondary, and "higher" education.

As a result of our uncritical acceptance of these two unexamined assumptions we have perpetuated a system of education in the American states which—for all of its strengths—is unduly fragmented internally and seriously out of touch with the political bases of its support.

To correct this educational isolation and fragmentation, we need not only a fresh viewpoint and a broader perspective, but concrete research data on the state-level educational/political situation.

The authors of this book, all three of them experienced students of both education and political science, have presented us here with a clear analysis of the interrelationships between elementary-secondary and higher education as these systems operate within the matrix of state politics in twelve of the most populous states. Their detailed study of these twelve states is specific, interesting, and insightful.

But the authors have taken another step beyond the merely descriptive and analytical: they have indicated alternatives for state action in revising governance patterns and financial support systems for public education at all levels.

In thus providing additional analyses and alternatives for consideration by education and political decision-makers in the states, the authors have performed a unique and a significant service to the American educational system.

Wendell H. Pierce
Executive Director,
Education Commission of the States

Contents

I. The Character of the Study   **1**

II. Profiles of the Relationship of Elementary-Secondary and Higher Education in Selected States   **11**

    California, 11
    Florida, 21
    Georgia, 33
    Illinois, 54
    Indiana, 65
    Massachusetts, 75
    Michigan, 90
    New Jersey, 100
    New York, 117
    Ohio, 132
    Pennsylvania, 142
    Texas, 153

III. Comparative Analysis of Some Major Elements in Interlevel Relations   **163**

Conclusion: Trends and Directions in Educational Policy-Making   **187**

1 | *The Character of the Study*

No one needs to be told today of the importance the American culture ascribes to education. Indeed, the nation's commitment to education as a means of fulfilling individual and social dreams is nearly as old as the culture itself. In recent years the society has shown itself ready to back up this commitment with massive investment in public educational institutions. The expenditure for the schools exceeds that for any other category of public outlay, excepting only national defense. With population continuing to grow and with the economy demanding higher levels of trained occupational specialization, it seems inevitable that these expenditures will continue to rise, both in absolute and in proportionate terms. It could be otherwise only in the event that international threats preempted even more public dollars than they now do, or if there were a sudden, major reversal of cultural values, or if new developments in technology and social organization suddenly made it possible to do the educational job more cheaply. None of these prospects seems likely to come about.

In these circumstances, it is interesting to take note of the basis on which the country's resources are allocated and organized for education. Perhaps no other term applies to the situation so well as "fragmented." Education is directed from three levels of government: local, state, and national. It is financed from a grab-bag of sources. In its most critical aspects it shows sharp variation from place to place, especially, but not exclusively, when those places are separated by state lines. Thus it is only in the most general sense that one can speak of an American educational system.

One of the most consequential of these lines of fragmentation divides education into elementary-secondary and higher education levels. The development of this sharp line of division, so well established that to most people it seems entirely natural, is an intriguing subject in itself, but it lies beyond the scope of our present interest. We are concerned with the consequences of the separation of levels at a time when a variety of new questions about the financing and operation of educational systems are being raised because of socio-political problems.

There seems to be no particular natural merit in the neat division of educational experience and institutions into compartments separated by the break between the twelfth and thirteenth grades. Arguments based on maturity, learning capacity, and the like are doubtful in the light of research, and similar cases can be made with apparently equal validity for a variety of other breaking points. Thus the distinction between the elementary-secondary and higher educational levels is one of usage, albeit usage with compelling effects.

Recently, various pressures have begun to bring into question the arbitrary division between these two educational spheres. One source of such pressure is the expanding cost of education at all levels, a consequence of growing enrollments and generally mounting prices. The expense to the state has, of course, been magnified as greater proportions of students in higher education have gone to public institutions. A second source of pressure has been the increasing propensity, on the part of many elements in society, to question the effectiveness of established educational forms and procedures, including traditional divisions between grade levels. Especially in the last decade, critics have raised a great variety of doubts about some of the rigidities of the American approach to schooling. Thirdly, the direction of social development has generated demands for educational services that overlap or fall between the traditional concerns of elementary-secondary and collegiate sectors, notably vocational-technical education and continuing adult education. As we shall try to demonstrate in the pages that follow, these and other, more particular factors have acted to bring the educational levels into closer relationship in most states.

In major ways, of course, as this relationship develops it becomes a political one. Education has always, in some sense, been an object of political action. The increasing importance of inter-level relations has added a new dimension to the politics of education in many places. Where elementary-secondary and higher education have traditionally been treated as separate fields of public policy, they are now more and more being seen as parts of the same area of problems. This change, of course, is not usually a stark one. It is induced by subtle forces, and it involves institutions long settled in their ways. The goal of the present study is to describe and evaluate the present state of the relationship between educational levels, and to examine the ways in which this relationship affects political processes and policies.

The questions we have tried to answer fall into three basic categories:

(1) *The form of the relationship.* What forms do these changes in relationship take? How are they felt by the people and institutions involved? Does the awareness of a relationship between educational levels vary from place to place and from institution to institution?

(2) *The processes affecting the relationship.* How is this relationship being handled in various places? To what extent does it take the form of conflict, to what extent the form of cooperation? What institutions are involved in dealing with it, and what institutions are being developed for the purpose?

(3) *Analysis of the relationship.* Why do these patterns differ as they do? What explanations can be adduced for the variety of phenomena uncovered in pursuing the questions mentioned above?

The unit of analysis used in this study is the state, as the state is the political arena where the critical decisions are made about educational programs and resources. The twelve states that constituted the sample are California, Florida, Georgia, Illinois, Indiana, Massachusetts, Michigan, New Jersey, New York, Ohio, Pennsylvania, and Texas. They include twelve of the fifteen most populous states, twelve of the thirteen with highest common school-age populations and twelve of the fourteen with the highest total (elementary-secondary and higher) school enrollments as of 1965. Well over half of Americans in each of these categories reside in the states studied. The sample includes, however, considerable variation in some pertinent characteristics. Among these are region, per capita wealth, socio-economic structure, growth, tradition, and political and educational organization. Thus the study was designed to provide information on the states that are most significant in terms of numbers, and at the same time to preserve the possibility of testing in a limited and exploratory way some interesting theoretical questions about the politics of education. While the size of the sample excludes any but the most tentative generalizations, its internal variation is such as to permit a preliminary approach to systematic analysis.

The research on which the report is based has drawn primarily on two sources of information: interviews and published documents. Interviews were held in each of the sample states with key informants selected by their institutional positions and by casual attributions of knowledge and influence. While the set of interviewees varied somewhat in composition from state to state, it usually included state education officials, officials of executive agencies including budget and finance officers, legislators and members of legislative staffs, leaders and staffs of education-related groups, knowledgeable citizens, and newspaper people. Among the respondents in all states were people from both elementary-secondary and higher education systems, from both public agencies and private organizations, and from both executive and legislative branches of state government. It cannot be said that coverage of any kind was assured by this approach, but most points of view were tapped and many sources of information utilized.

The interviews were rather undirected in nature, but structured around a set of basic inquiries. Before interviewing was started a list of questions was devised, and this served as a guide and check-list for discussions with respondents, the specific order and content being tailored to the role of the interviewee. This procedure seemed appropriate to the exploratory nature of the research. Here, too, as with the selection of the sample, the design of the project limited its capacity to produce systematic generalization, but it provided maximum opportunity to map out the pertinent issues and relationships in each of the states studied.

Supplementary evidence has been culled from a variety of official reports, statistical documents, staff studies, and other relevant materials. Some research was also done with newspapers in the subject states. Obviously, the range of possibly valuable sources is endless, and only a small portion of them could be touched within the limits of this study.

As preface to the body of the report, it may be helpful to outline the principal issues, processes, and institutions that comprise the political relationships of elementary-secondary and higher education. The content and mix of these elements vary from state to state, but the broad categories remain the same. These constitute the structure of the project design. In keeping with the exploratory nature of the work, they were in part derived from some pre-theory about the nature of political relationships and in part induced from the body of evidence and experience accumulated as the research progressed.

Basically, our evidence can be grouped into three clusters of variables, as follows:

(1) *Environment*. Recent research on state and local politics has suggested that some aspects of the environment have substantial effects on the way systems work. As was pointed out above, the design of this project permitted some consideration of such factors, though we have not dealt with them and indeed could not do so in a comprehensive and systematic way. Environment, of course, is a term that can cover a great range of conditions, many of which might be expected to influence the course of educational politics. In terms of their theoretical relevance, these factors may be thought of as the conditions out of which demands on the political system are generated, and the conditions that define the society's (in this case the state's) capacity to support public services. Any number of indexes of environment have been used in political analysis, including such things as population, sex, age distribution, region (a mix of social and cultural factors), wealth, distribution of wealth, industrialization, and urbanization. These serve, in a loose sense, as the independent variables in our design.

(2) *Political institutions and processes.* The focal point of the project has been the institutions and processes of educational politics themselves. Here the relationship of elementary-secondary and higher education is manifested in the interactions of persons and groups. Pertinent institutions include those involved in the general business of making decisions for the state, namely, legislatures and their staffs, governors, budget and finance agencies, etc. They also include those charged with the government of education such as state boards, departments of education, boards of regents, coordinating councils, and related bodies. Our fundamental questions are how these individuals and organizations behave when they deal with policy that brings the two levels of the educational system together, and why they behave as they do. The answer must take into consideration the activities of private education-related groups and such organs of power as political parties seen against a background of political culture and educational tradition. Out of evidence about these various elements of politics—structures of authority, decision-making processes, and sources and modes of influence—we have tried to construct comparative accounts of similarities and differences in the handling of educational problems. Specifically, of course, our interest has been directed at the handling of issues where the interests of elementary-secondary and higher education meet.

(3) *The critical issues.* The interests of elementary-secondary and higher education tend at present to converge on a small number of critical problems. It is chiefly through the stimulus provided by these issues that the two levels come into contact and develop systems of conflict and/or cooperation. These issues take different shape in various states, and they are perceived and processed differently from place to place. But the substance of relationship between the two levels of education quite consistently revolves around this limited set of policy questions. Like the institutions of decision-making in educational politics, these, then, have been central points of reference in our investigations.

More specifically, four categories of policy problems may be said to stand in this position:

(A) *Fiscal questions.* As we pointed out earlier, the pressures of social demand on education are primarily felt through expanding financial needs. Both elementary-secondary and higher education have seen costs grow enormously in recent years. Typically, the two sectors have drawn on somewhat different sources of support, the public schools having been heavily dependent on local real property taxes and the colleges and universities drawing their monies directly from the state, from student fees, and from federal grants and contracts. As costs have risen, however, and particularly as the tax burden on real estate has come to seem unreasonable, the schools and colleges have increasingly turned for aid to the same source: general state revenues. They have come into competition, sometimes overt but more often unspoken, for larger shares out of a common but limited pot of money. This trend has also had the effect of throwing more and more of the decisions about finance on both levels into the same decision-making arenas, the state legislatures. In these ways, fiscal problems have generated inter-level relationships.

(B) *Education in 13th and 14th grades.* With the expansion of demand for education beyond the high school, a variety of patterns have grown for handling the 13th and 14th grades. Two kinds of needs are encountered at this level, the need for terminal programs in certain kinds of fields, and the need for academic programs suitable to prepare students for junior-year entry into the college or university. As higher education has been sought by larger numbers of students, pressure has mounted to provide 13th and 14th grade opportunities near to home and on a basis that is economical both for individual students and the state.

Responses to these pressures have varied, but the two basic patterns have been the junior-community college system and the branch campus device, with some states using a combination. The entire problem raises issues of institutional control, orientation, and finance. In some states the 13th and 14th grade programs have been grafted onto the public schools and chiefly promoted and dominated by public school interests. In others, the major initiative has come from higher education, and in some a pattern has yet to develop. In nearly every situation, however, the elementary-secondary and higher education people have been participants in the political processes of decision-making on the questions involved.

(C) *Vocational-technical education.* Provision of opportunities for vocational-technical education has raised problems similar to, and in some cases intertwined with, those discussed in connection with the 13th and 14th grades. Vocational-technical training appears to have been a stepchild of the American educational system. It lacks the prestige of academic programs, and its potential clientele is increasingly drawn (with the decline of vocational agriculture) from less powerful groups in society. The demand for vocational programs changes as the needs of business and industry evolve. Also, the age-groups which vocational-technical education serves range from high-schoolers to adults in middle-age who need "retooling."

The unevenness of the vocational education field is reflected in its dispersion among a variety of institutions in most states. Commonly, some programs are offered by high schools on a pregraduation and continuation basis, some are housed in special schools, and some in colleges and universities. In many places there is little in the way of coordination and no political cohesion among the various vocational-technical training efforts. The difficulty of defining the field in thoroughly clear and acceptable terms and the fact that it ordinarily has no traditional institutional focus have brought it into the sphere of interlevel relationships. Vocational education overlaps both secondary and higher school programs, but neither sector has customarily accepted it as a real responsibility. Thus it tends to linger in the shadows between the two levels, not fully a part of either.

(D) *Teacher training and certification.* The fourth major question on which elementary-secondary and higher education tend to find themselves in confrontation is that of the training of public school teachers. This is specifically, of course, the job of the colleges and universities. However, the teacher training institutions have long had close ties with the practicing educational profession, and the latter has had a great influence over entry requirements. In effect, the arrangement has been that of a guild.

This relationship is no longer so firm. One reason is that the teachers colleges have virtually disappeared as specialized institutions, most having developed liberal arts programs and moved under the control of state higher education systems. As they are no longer distinct institutional entities, they are no longer so easily subject to the influence of the profession. In addition, the recent blossoming of interest in education in general has had repercussions on teacher education. The scholarly world and the legislatures have paid more attention to the preparation of teachers and raised more questions about the requirements of certification. In some instances these matters have assumed the status of a "cause," and nearly everywhere the rise in concern about teacher training has brought about a higher level of interaction between the public schools and the world of higher education. This interaction has often been of a highly political nature and fairly often it has resulted in explicitly political decisions.

The importance of our subject is manifest in the discussion above. The individuals, groups, and agencies of educational decision-making in the states, acting on the issues reviewed and on others, have gravitated toward treating education from lowest to highest as a single subject of policy and planning. The gravitation has, however, been slow, often unconscious, and often resisted. A great many factors in the established system of educational politics mitigate against the development of a single outlook for all school problems.

One thing seems certain: the pressures toward political interaction of elementary-secondary and higher education will increase in the years ahead. The fiscal squeeze alone seems sufficient to bring further evolution in this direction. It is not our purpose to promote a given course of action or a given institutional change. However, we are confident of two things: these developments can be ignored only at considerable peril to education; and the common sharing, comparing, and evaluating of experience is a step toward confronting problems on a realistic basis. Unless the nature of the interlevel relationship is brought to overt consciousness, wasteful conflict seems likely to result, and opportunities for more effective educational action will be missed. Resources will continue to be allocated on a piecemeal basis, programs will lack coordination, and decision-makers will operate with small pieces of the total picture in view. It is our hope that this study might in some small way help put the government of all education on a more rational basis.

2 | Profiles of the Relationship of Elementary-Secondary and Higher Education in Selected States

The purpose of this chapter is to present, in abbreviated form, collected data concerning each of the twelve states studied. An attempt has been made to extract the major factors affecting the interlevel relationship in education in each of the states. In so doing, it has not been possible to capture the detail that exists in the original, unpublished twelve state reports that provide the basis for the summaries that follow. This exclusion of much of the detail may limit the cohesion of this chapter and the scholarly character of the report, but it should not impair the usefulness of the findings.

This chapter is divided into twelve sections with the states presented alphabetically, one per section. The subsections under most states will include (1) the organization of education, (2) the crucial issues involving the interlevel relationship, and (3) some conclusions and predictions about the future. The following profiles, it should be noted, take account of the ever-changing educational situation in the subject states only through the summer of 1967.

I. CALIFORNIA

California is unique in many respects. Its size, growth, social heterogeneity, and political tradition set it apart and tend to discourage efforts to compare it with other states. Its political climate has characteristically been one of ambiguity and ferment. On closer examination, however, this uniqueness is only superficial. Every state develops its own political subculture, its distinctive patterns of rhetoric and relationships, and these differences often have substantial effects. But the underlying processes and problems are much alike from state to state. Thus, except for some small variations, the relationship between elementary-secondary and higher education in California and in other states is basically the same. The important differences may have more to do with stages of development and styles of discussion than with fundamental problems. This is probably the most important factor to note in a discussion of the educational situation in California.

The relationship between elementary-secondary and higher education in California is quiet but potentially explosive. There are points of competition and conflict, and there have been some, but relatively few, efforts at coordination. Several factors would seem to raise the probabilities of conflict in the near future. The growth in the state's population has put tremendous pressure on the education system at all levels, particularly in the area of demand for capital investment, which will be difficult to meet and hard to postpone or ignore. In one form or another this is bound to become a source of political controversy. At the same time, California has a traditional commitment to education that legitimizes these pressures. This commitment is manifest in the nation's best-developed junior college system. Control of that system is in itself an object of potential controversy, because of its involvement with long-established interests. The major contestants for influence in education in California are traditionally powerful but at present are fragmented and defensive. The coordinative device for higher education lacks tools and experience; the forces of elementary-secondary education have difficulty in keeping pace with the pressures of change. Thus the ingredients of conflict, issues and political fluidity, are much in evidence.

This is not to say, however, that such conflict is an active part of the picture of educational politics in California. Generalized conflict between elementary-secondary and higher education is not openly apparent and its presence is usually doubted or denied by people involved in politics. There are, of course, current concrete issues that cut across levels, notably fiscal questions and questions about the organization and control of junior college and vocational-technical education. These, however, are not usually defined in terms of the elementary-secondary and higher education relationship. They tend to be seen as discrete and fairly specific problems, and often as problems relevant to one level or another even when they are clearly of broader reach. Thus, the overall relationship is concealed in traditional definitions and categories and treated within the complex interplay of multiple political forces.

The Organization of Education

The government of elementary-secondary education

Like most states, California has its own distinctive and rather cumbersome pattern of organization for the government of elementary and secondary education. The central institutions are a State Board and a State Department of Education.

The Board is a body of ten lay members appointed for four-year staggered terms by the governor with the approval of two-thirds of the Senate. It is presumably the policy-making and monitoring body for the educational system, including the junior colleges but no longer including the state college system. The Department of Education is headed by a state superintendent elected by the people of the state on a formally non-partisan basis for a four-year term. The superintendent is both the executive officer of the board and the operating head of a large department charged with responsibility for carrying out state school policies.

This arrangement clearly bears the seeds of confusion, conflict, and ambiguity of leadership. Until the late 1950's the board and superintendent apparently got on quite amicably and neither led a very vigorous political life. Then many things began to change. The flight of Sputnik sent reverberations throughout

American education. The fiscal situation in California began to tighten, but the growth of the state continued at a fantastic pace. The twelve-year tenure of the state superintendent came to an end. And the culmination of several years of preparation brought adoption of the Master Plan for Higher Education and ensuing alteration of the relationship of the board and department to higher education.

These and other developments had a variety of short and long run consequences for the government of education in California. Just what is cause and what is effect cannot be untangled here. It is apparent, however, that the period of comfort and amicability died somewhere along the line. The governor appointed to the Board of Education several people who did not fit into the traditional mold of board behavior. They are variously described by various people; for our purposes it will suffice to say that they seem to have desired a more active policy-making role for the board and were inclined to be skeptical of the approaches to educational policy advanced by the professional educators. Meanwhile, the superintendency was won in a bitter campaign in 1962 by a controversial man who aspires to higher political office.

The superintendent and the board have frequently been at odds over the past few years, sometimes in quite open conflict. Both have also been in conflict on a variety of issues with a substantial share of the state's professional educators. The more or less routine functions of the Department of Education seem to have gone forward much as before, and the department itself has apparently not experienced a major organizational shake-up.

From the standpoint of the elementary-secondary and higher education relationship, the main consequence of this set of developments seems to have been the loss of cohesion and sense of thrust by the various forces identified with elementary-secondary education. Leadership is lacking or diffused, and "education" seems to speak with many voices. A correlative and perhaps contributing factor has been the loss of some prestige and power by the California Teachers Association (CTA).

The causes of this change can be no more than a matter of speculation here. In good part it probably grows out of the difficulties a heavily organized and bureaucratized (the latter term is meant in a non-pejorative sense) group commonly has in staying at the frontier of a rapidly changing field. It also doubtless reflects the lethargy of a profession, long encouraged not to rock the boat, confronted with accelerating, and often conflicting, social demands for change.

Several specific factors seem to have been responsible for the changes described. The CTA has been under growing pressure from the union movement, especially in the urban areas. It has traditionally tended to be strong in rural and smaller communities, but with the union threat and legislative reapportionment coming almost simultaneously, the disposition of political forces in education has been subtly altered. Meanwhile, more attention has been given to higher education. The CTA has had only token influence and support in this field. Furthermore, in 1961 the CTA lost a furious battle over legislation (the Fisher Act) to make substantial changes in teacher certification requirements. Many of the wounds suffered in this encounter by various groups have not yet healed completely.

The government of higher education

The present government of higher education has been shaped from a tradition of commitment, a record of fantastic growth, and great efforts to keep up with the demand. Historically, the University of California has stood at the center of higher education in the state. The state college system is a later development. This system is comprised of several former teacher-training institutions along with a number of entirely new campuses. Until recently it was under the direction of the State Board of Education and the State Superintendent. Thus it had a built-in link with elementary-secondary school interests, which apparently is of little importance except perhaps as it relates to its teacher-training function.

After an extensive joint study of California's needs in higher education, the legislature directed the preparation of a Master Plan which was enacted into policy in 1960. One of its major consequences was the separation of the state colleges from the

Board of Education and creation of a Board of Trustees for the state college system. In addition, among other things, the Master Plan provided guidelines for the division of functions among university, state colleges, and the junior colleges, and established a Coordinating Council for Higher Education. The Coordinating Council has been acclaimed as California's answer to the problem of coordinating a large and diffuse set of higher education institutions. In effect, the council is an advisory organization. It may request information from institutions and comment on the level of budgetary support sought, but it has no further control over allocations. It reviews proposals for new academic programs but here, again, its powers are in effect advisory.

At present, the Coordinating Council is probably best defined as a developing force in the politics of higher education. Observers comment that it is increasingly making itself heard with the legislature and governor, but its formal role is not strong and its ultimate influence untested. The current situation should encourage much growth, however, because many of the traditional elements in the picture are changing. The university, once unquestionably the main unit in the system, has declined in power. Concurrent with the decline in influence of the university has been a rapid growth of the state college.

The position of the junior colleges with respect to the state political situation will be reviewed later. Excluding them for the moment, the educational system in California may be considered to be in a state of flux. Older lines of influence and alliance are no longer firm, and competition among the components is noteworthy. The Coordinating Council is at present more a third force than a predominant integrating influence. The fragmentation of the system in a setting of political controversy and change makes it impossible for higher education to act as a coherent participant in the processes of state politics.

Some Major Issues

The developing relations between elementary-secondary and higher education in California can best be demonstrated in the discussion of specific issues that cut across levels.

The fiscal problem

Traditionally, California has been generous with education. It ranks high among the states in providing funds and promoting interest in both public higher education and the public schools. Its ability and willingness to pay is reinforced by a dynamic economy. Current political trends suggest, however, that the situation may be worsening, a development which could adversely affect interlevel relationships.

State support for higher education is provided through lump-sum legislative appropriations for the university and the various state colleges from the general fund.

In some degree, this fiscal independence of the higher education systems has been tempered by the establishment of the Coordinating Council. While judgments must be tentative, the effect of the Council's existence so far may have been to reduce the total power of the university and state college system without replacing it with comparable political force on the integrated or overall level. Thus the Council might be used as a convenient device against the component institutions until it develops the power to protect them.

Fiscal developments in the elementary-secondary field also make a change in basic relationships likely, though the specific problems are quite different. As in other states, public school finance in California is the joint responsibility of the state government and the local school districts. The state's share, apportioned through a foundation program which provides a minimum amount of state aid for each district, consists of a flat grant plus a variable amount calculated by an equalization formula. At the level of state politics two principal processes are concerned. One is periodic consideration and adjustment by the legislature and governor of the foundation program. The second is the routine appropriation of money from the general fund to the common school fund in an amount adequate to cover foundation program requirements.

California's level of state aid to local districts is high compared with those of other states, but pressure to raise it is as unremitting in California as elsewhere. Another element in the situation is the growing pressure for relief from rising property taxes.

The junior college financial situation is roughly comparable to that of the elementary and secondary schools. Until recently their total support came from the local taxing districts. In the last few years the state has provided some capital outlay funds, but operating expenditures are still derived from local sources. There is substantial pressure to change the entire structure of junior college control. Such a change might involve a regular system of state aid, or even, if the most sweeping proposals were adopted, complete state support.

From the standpoint of the development of the interlevel relationship, these trends and possibilities are important for what they might do to educational politics. Education as a whole is the largest single item of state expenditure in California; indeed, it accounts for more than half of all general fund dollars spent. In any move to cut public spending or hold it steady, education is likely to suffer. The levels of education have to date usually been treated as separate spheres. One may wonder, however, if this will continue to be the case if elementary-secondary education and perhaps the junior colleges are made more dependent on general fund appropriations through adoption and extension of tax relief plans. These moves might well have the effect of breaking down the separation of public school and public higher education finance and increasing the probability of competition between the various factions for the state's tax dollar.

The junior colleges and vocational-technical education

California has to determine the direction post-high school education should take, where the responsibility for post-high school education should lie, and where this function will fit into the future educational program. There are now some 78 junior colleges in the state, many with sizeable enrollments and many of considerable age. The junior colleges are under local control, in some cases the operating heads being the superintendents of local school districts. Financial support is substantially local. Until a few years ago the junior colleges were financed entirely from local district resources. Recently there have been some subventions for capital development and about 30% of the total operating budgets are supplied by the state through a foundation program.

For historical reasons, the junior colleges have traditionally been identified with high school interests. The Donahue Act, however, formally designated the junior colleges as part of the state's higher education system. This declaration was symbolic of some of the pressures for change. Questions are now raised, out of the plethora of complex issues, as to whether the entire structure should be revised. These involve matters of local control, of state organization, and of financing of the junior colleges.

The first question is whether part, or all, of the control of the junior colleges should be taken out of the hands of local boards and vested in some state agency. The state's junior college program has been managed piecemeal by several bureaus of the State Department of Education, but in the 1967 session the legislature transferred these functions to a new Board of Governors of the California Community Colleges. The Board will have responsibility for state-level junior college policy and will appoint an executive officer. The legislation reaffirms the local autonomy and identity of the colleges, and presumably does not therefore substantially alter the existing distribution of functions. This reorganization is a major step in the evolution of higher education in California, but its full implications cannot yet be forecast.

These comments illustrate the ambiguities of the position of the junior colleges in educational politics. The point is not that the junior colleges are prizes sought after by competing elementary-secondary and higher education interests. The situation is not that rational. Rather, junior college programs and control are problems that involve many of the issues, symbolic and concrete, that tend to excite controversy among educational interests. To some degree these are the kinds of issues that contribute to the polarization of the educational community. As such they may crystallize conflict between levels as they are debated, or they may serve as catalysts in bringing levels together by dramatizing convergencies of interest and concern.

The problem of vocational-technical education is intertwined with the matter of the role of the junior colleges. The issues are not clean-cut, and the background is highly complicated. In California the job of providing such education has been divided between the junior colleges and the secondary schools. At the present time this division of responsibility is an irritant to the relationship between the two departments but once this problem is solved the future for vocational-technical education can be limitless.

Teacher credentials

Teacher accrediting is a complicated and touchy issue. It provided the focus of a great educational furor in California in 1961, climaxed by the passage of the Fisher Act. This legislation, fiercely opposed by the CTA, turned credential requirements in a more academic direction. The 1961 issue revolved around the question of whether the colleges or elementary-secondary education institutions should determine the curriculum for preparation of school teachers. The Fisher Act, favoring the colleges, is still controversial in California and various professional groups are trying to amend it. Their efforts do not appear, however, to be major items on the agenda of educational politics. Most interested persons seem to be able to live with the Fisher Act.

Educational Decision-Making

The role of the legislature in educational decision-making has been strengthened by conflict among the CTA, the State Board, and the State Department of Education. It is also strengthened by the fact that the university has lost political influence, the state colleges have not gained a comparable power, and the Coordinating Council has only limited tools for functioning efficiently, is untested, and is still developing. Thus the legislature no longer feels the pressure it once did from these sources, and it no longer looks to them with confidence for advice.

At the same time the legislature itself has developed strong leadership, some of it with special interest in the education field. The division of seats between the parties in the House has been close, and recent campaigns for Governor and State Superintendent have been highly partisan. These facts have probably whetted the legislative appetite to act on educational issues, for the intrinsic importance of education along with the fiscal squeeze have made it more than ever a powerful, if ambiguous, political subject.

From an analytic point of view the consequences of this legislative predominance might go either of two ways. The legislature is, along with the governor, the final repository of state authority and therefore the ultimate coordinating body for education. It is also the central focus of fiscal decision-making. By custom it handles educational matters at all levels through a common set of committees, the education and finance committees of House and Senate. It is perhaps the ideal body to coordinate educational programs and distribute resources, especially given aid from the executive branch.

On the other hand, there are reasons not to depend on the legislature as a truly effective coordinating institution for education. While the California legislature is relatively well-staffed and well-paid, and while it meets fairly often, it is doubtful that it can generate an integrated approach to policy-making. Its membership is deluged under a flood of proposals on a tremendous variety of subjects. The problems of legislative effectiveness, shared by all states, are magnified in California by the size of the state, its heterogeneity, and again, the pace of change, all of which create issues difficult to manage.

One might expect, therefore, that unless or until some substantial organizational change or political crystallization develops in California, educational affairs are likely to be handled in a piecemeal fashion. If this is the case, the threats and opportunities inherent in the relationship between elementary-secondary and higher education are likely to go unnoticed and untended, except when they burst into specific issue conflicts.

II. FLORIDA

The Organization of Education in Florida

Knowledge of the unique governmental structure of Florida is essential to understanding state decision-making patterns in education. The state is governed under an unusual plural executive system. Six independently elected constitutional officials share administrative powers with the governor. This cabinet consists of the governor, the secretary of state, the attorney-general, the state treasurer, the comptroller, the commissioner of agriculture, and the state superintendent of public instruction. These seven elected officials serve on a large number of *ex officio* boards which are responsible for making major budgetary, purchasing, and personnel decisions in the state. These cabinet boards exercise enormous influence and oversee major policy areas such as education, conservation, and safety.

As a member of a host of influential and overlapping boards, each cabinet member enjoys considerable political power and influence. The Superintendent of Public Instruction, in addition to his obvious duties as chief school officer, serves as a member of the state board of education and on thirteen other state boards responsible for important policy areas that would ordinarily be considered beyond the purview of the professional educator. The Superintendent of Public Instruction thus has influence in many policy areas that extend beyond the bounds of education. Most students of government both within and outside the state have criticized the cabinet system as being archaic, confusing to the public, cumbersome, and inefficient in its operation.

Students of state educational structures likewise react negatively to the Florida system. Floridians in positions of educational leadership, however, point to the fact that the Superintendent of Public Instruction has great political leverage as a cabinet member. Each member of the cabinet has equal voting power. The Superintendent of Public Instruction can use this power to obtain support for desired educational programs in exchange for his support of matters of interest to other cabinet members. Supporters of the Florida educational structure also cite the advantages of having one constitutionally created State Board of Education responsible for coordinating the entire spectrum of publicly supported education from kindergarten through graduate school.

The superintendent's position within the cabinet structure is also strengthened by the fact that all his colleagues as elected officials are vitally interested in the school vote. A politically sophisticated state superintendent of public instruction, well integrated into the cabinet's *modus operandi* and enjoying the respect and confidence of his fellow cabinet officers, can exercise enormous educational leadership.

The State Board of Education in Florida exercises control over every level of public education. Although Florida has a State Board of Regents responsible for administering the public universities, this board is still responsible to the State Board of Education which exercises final approval of policies, rules, and regulations adopted by the Board of Regents. The State Board must also approve each gubernatorial appointment to the nine-member Board of Regents, all academic salaries of $15,000 per annum and over, the selection of the chief executive officer of the Board of Regents, the president of each institution, and the head of each agency in the state university system.

The state constitution designates that the Board of Education should consist of the governor, the secretary of state, the attorney-general, the state treasurer, and the state superintendent of public instruction.

The Board of Regents which, as stated above, is responsible to the State Board of Education was established by the legislature in 1965 to supervise the activities of the rapidly growing state university system. The nine members, appointed by the governor and approved by the Board of Education, must be confirmed by the legislature. They are subject to removal for any cause on the concurrence of a majority of the State Board of Education.

In recent years the university-level components under the control of the Board of Regents have grown from three units to seven units and student attendance has more than doubled the 50,000 enrollment recorded in 1957. In order to cope with this phenomenal growth, the Board of Regents and its Chancellor have been delegated increased authority to coordinate budgets and plan curricula for the constituent institutions of the university system.

Despite the increased responsibilities which the Regents have assumed in recent years, there is still much dissatisfaction with the way university decision-making is structured at the state level. There is no clear-cut division in the respective roles and responsibilities of the State Board of Education and the Board of Regents. The structural system through which Florida's public universities are administered is criticized as being inadequate to the needs of a rapidly expanding system of public universities. There is need to clarify various board relationships, functions, and structures within the university system.

There appears to be little formal inter-board consultation. Constitutionally, the Superintendent of Public Instruction is responsible for all public education including the universities. However, this legal responsibility for higher education has not been exercised seriously. The Superintendent of Public Instruction focuses his attention and the work of the Department of Public Instruction upon matters involving elementary-secondary and junior college education and has refrained from involvement in university administration.

It appears also that there has been very little consultation at the staff level between members of the Department of Public Instruction and the Regents' staff. For the most part, the operations are quite distinct, with the Regents' staff focusing its energies upon university issues and the State Board of Education's Department of Public Instruction devoting almost exclusive attention to elementary, secondary, and junior college education.

Organizations like the Florida Education Association (FEA) have been too concerned with the many problems confronting the public schools to allocate substantial staff time to issues relating to higher education. They maintain relationships with representatives of higher education only on an *ad hoc* basis.

There has been organized at the state level a professional committee to coordinate the plans and programs of the various levels of public education in Florida. Representatives from schools and colleges throughout the state serve on this committee which focuses most of its attention upon coordinating the general education programs of the junior colleges and universities. This is an increasingly important function as more and more junior college students transfer to the universities. The committee spends little time coordinating high school and post-high school programs.

The Department of Public Instruction is responsible for coordinating and supervising Florida's growing junior colleges which have become such an influential educational and political force in the state. The growth of the community-centered junior colleges in Florida has been little short of phenomenal. As enrollments soared and the needs of the junior colleges became apparent, a Community College Council was established in the mid 1950's to blueprint a master plan for junior college development in Florida. The master plan projected that a community-centered junior college education should be available within commuting distance from home for every Florida youngster. There are at the time of this writing community colleges within commuting distance from the homes of more than 80% of Florida's young people.

The Division of Community Junior Colleges appears to exercise considerable autonomy. Structurally under the control of the Superintendent of Public Instruction, the Division of Community Junior Colleges is not only physically separated from the Department of Public Instruction but operationally has much freedom. The Director of the Division has his own staff, reports to his own Advisory Board, and employs separate fiscal and academic officers for the junior colleges. The Division, however, commonly does utilize the various administrative, research, vocational, and technical services of the Department.

There is no overt conflict between the rapidly growing junior colleges and the universities. The Board of Regents with its exclusive university responsibilities has no desire to operate the junior colleges. There have been several recent efforts to separate the junior colleges from Florida's county school system, but these efforts have failed since officials manifest little or no desire to incorporate the junior colleges into the university system.

The State Department of Public Instruction, in addition to its responsibilities for junior colleges, also operates vocational and technical centers. These centers have generated considerable controversy in Florida as they have in other states we have visited. Most of the controversy revolved around the establishment of separate vocational and technical centers instead of incorporating them into already established junior colleges to avoid duplication and waste. The controversy was resolved by locating new vocational and technical centers on existing junior college or high school property or by sharing the physical plant of existing junior colleges or high schools where such facilities were available. In areas without such facilities, separate vocational and technical centers were built.

The separate vocational and technical centers which have been so recently established for out-of-school youth and adults are under the supervision of a special officer in the Department of Public Instruction. The vocational and technical centers that are located in junior colleges are supervised by the Director of the Division of Junior Colleges.

Some Major Issues

Budget preparation and presentation

There are three separate public educational budgets presented in Florida: one for the elementary and secondary schools, one for the junior colleges, and a third for the universities. The budget for the elementary and secondary schools is developed by the Department of Public Instruction, usually in close consultation with the Florida Education Association. State expenditures for public education are allocated on a formula basis predicated on teachers' salaries. The research branch of the Department of Public Instruction is constantly working on the basic state aid formula to insure adequate support to school systems confronted with additional expenditures caused by burgeoning enrollments, inflation, and demands for educational improvement. Recent outbreaks of teacher militancy have had significant implications for Florida because the state aid formula is predicated on salaries developed cooperatively by the Department and the FEA. The teachers' organization usually has higher demands for the schools than the Superintendent of Public Instruction. The latter, as a popularly elected state official, must remain sensitive to his responsibility to the taxpayer as well as to the teacher in formulating his position on state aid. Recent events have placed an unprecedented strain on the traditional alliance between the Department of Public Instruction and the FEA.

The state junior college budget is also developed by the Department of Public Instruction. Beginning in 1957, foundation aid funds for the junior colleges were appropriated and administered separately in accord with recommendations made by the Community College Council. The basic support formula for the junior colleges was differentiated from the foundation program utilized to finance the elementary and secondary schools.

Despite the separate state aid formula and the fact that since 1957 each junior college has computed and administered its budget separately from that of its county school system, junior college budgets must be approved by the county school board. These boards have no additional source of local revenue beyond the local school tax. If local communities desired to support junior colleges more generously, conflict with the county public schools would be likely to occur. Approximately 10% of junior college expenditures are normally derived from local sources.

The Board of Regents now has the responsibility of coordinating the university budgets. Since 1967, the Regents staff has been responsible for reviewing the individual university budgets and preparing a single budgetary request for the university system.

The State Budget Commission is not mentioned in the Florida Constitution but it has statutory authority and great influence. The membership of the State Budget Commission is identical with that of the State Board of Education. The Budget Commission has the statutory power and responsibility to review and revise, if necessary, the financial requests of state agencies including those of the educational institutions. Final approval rests in the hands of the legislature.

The Superintendent of Public Instruction, of course, is intimately involved with elementary and secondary education as well as junior college budget-making through the work of his department. As a member of the Budget Commission which controls all budgets, he is the sole educator in a position to pass judgment on the relative needs of the various levels.

There have been several moves to make the Board of Regents

independent of the Budget Commission. Representatives of the universities fear that the Budget Commission is oriented in favor of the public schools and community colleges. The public school people fear just the opposite. Despite the respective fears of representatives of both the public schools and higher education there has been no overt budgetary conflict between the levels of education.

The legislature in Florida is responsible for the final approval of budgets for educational institutions, but its sessions are so short and infrequent (60 days every other year) that it must rely heavily on outside guidance. The committees responsible for appropriations and fiscal matters are severely understaffed, and cannot develop the expertise essential to the intelligent appraisal of these budgets. For help with the elementary and secondary schools and the junior colleges, the legislators depend on information from the Department of Public Instruction and the FEA. The staff of the Board of Regents provides advice on the budgets of the state universities.

Some Perceptions of Florida's Educational Situation

Interviews with members of the legislature, educators at all levels, and other public and private officials evoked the following commonly accepted perceptions of the Florida educational situation:

(1) The establishment of the Board of Regents as a coordinating agency for the public universities was an encouraging development but the board was having difficulty in asserting itself because of the powerful political position of some universities.

(2) Junior colleges exert a particularly powerful political influence in Florida. They are well dispersed geographically throughout the state, offer opportunities for higher education within commuting range of most of the state's youngsters, and are politically buttressed by powerful local support.

(3) There is some resentment of junior college political influence by public school officials who feel that the great growth of junior colleges has diverted monies that should have been al-

located to meet the pressing needs of elementary and secondary schools.

(4) The universities also are apprehensive about the great growth of junior college influence because of their fears of possible direct competition for available resources.

(5) Legislators particularly fear that issues which are largely covert now may become more overt as the demands for education intensify at all levels and competition for scarce resources grows. Educational expenditures must be carefully assessed and legislators interviewed contend that they must reserve the final right to determine the allocation of resources.

The Florida Education Association is considered the most influential private group in determining educational policy. The FEA focuses much of its activity at the local and state level on legislation affecting teachers and public schools, including the junior colleges. University personnel, fearing loss of prestige or autonomy if linked too closely with the public schools, are wary of the FEA.

The powerful organization representing county school superintendents has traditionally worked closely with the FEA and has availed itself in the past of office space and staff services offered by the FEA. Recent and unprecedented teacher militancy, however, has created tensions between the FEA and other groups and individuals concerned with public education. Some of the traditional cooperative arrangements have been undergoing significant change. Differences between the organizations were so serious that the county superintendents' organization at the time this was written was considering breaking away from the FEA completely. The Florida School Boards Association also has split sharply with the FEA over some significant issues.

The Continuing Educational Council of Florida, composed of the president and one other member of each of 22 major statewide organizations with diversified interests, has traditionally allied itself with the FEA. Recent FEA activities, however, have weakened the unity of this coalition by alienating certain groups usually supportive of FEA positions on elementary and secondary education.

There is fear that continued erosion of the public school coalition will isolate the FEA and weaken substantially the political leverage of elementary-secondary education at a crucial time when competition for scarce resources will be getting progressively keener.

Some Impressions and Projections

Although there is little evidence of overt conflict between levels of education, the possibility of such conflict in the very near future is real. Despite the fact that expenditures for public schools, junior colleges, and universities are viewed as different, non-competitive budgetary propositions, much fear and suspicion exist that as tax assessments increase, the several educational levels will be competing for the same tax dollars in the general revenue fund.

Florida's politicians, like their colleagues in many other states, are extremely tax-sensitive at this time. The recent assessment reforms with the resultant increases in *ad valorem* taxation have stirred up a statewide storm. Some property taxes have tripled in just a few years. It is logical to assume that increases in local property taxes which heavily support the public schools and junior colleges have reached the saturation point. Increased expenditures for these levels of education for the foreseeable future may be available only from the state's general revenue fund which finances the universities.

For the first time then, there may well be competition for funds from the same source of revenue. Organizational spokesmen for the public school interests claimed that the property tax was already excessively high and emphasized that additional revenues would have to be provided by state-level taxation. One would imagine that the universities view with some apprehension the possibility that other levels of education might have access to general revenue funds.

The universities already feel that current state support is not adequate to meet their needs. For example, for the 1965–67 biennium the university system received only $136.9 million of $184 million asked for in operating funds and only $71.2 million of a requested $183 million in funds for capital outlay. The displeasure of the FEA with the low tax philosophy of the Florida legislature has been manifested quite dramatically in recent months.

Despite overtly harmonious personal relationships between leaders of the various educational levels in Florida, there are many suspicions and fears. These apprehensions were accentuated several years ago when the Board of Regents submitted to the State Board of Education a budgetary request that would have almost doubled the expenditures of the university system. This budgetary request, called "preposterous" by one public school spokesman, was sent back to the Regents with the request that a revamped budget be prepared which would set forth priorities and areas where the need for funds was most acute.

This budgetary request evidently stunned many educators as well as legislators. Public school people have been increasingly wary of the university system's great growth and influence, but have had their fears allayed by the fact the elementary and secondary schools except during the 1965 "no tax session" have fared rather well financially with the legislature. The fact that every educational level prior to 1965 felt that it had received at least a proportionate share of available revenue probably has been a major reason for the lack of conflict.

The elementary and secondary schools are, in a sense, running scared. They fear that the junior colleges and universities can "outpolitic" them. The programs in higher education are more prestigious, broadly gauged, and attractive. The universities command the loyalty of influential alumni. Graduates of the university law, medical, and business schools are very frequently leaders in the state's economic and civic as well as political life. Higher education thus enjoys prestige and influence that cannot be emulated by elementary and secondary schools and as a result fares better in the political arenas. Although some observers believe that the newly reapportioned and more urbanized legislature will be less susceptible to university blandishments than its predecessors, a feeling of political insecurity *vis-à-vis* higher education afflicted some of the spokesmen for Florida's elementary and secondary schools.

The public school people also feel that the universities have an advantage in terms of the way financial support for education is channeled in Florida. For example, when the universities submit their budgets requesting salary increments there is no need to go to the tax conscious legislature for a liberalization of the basic formula. The universities can derive the desired resources through political action drawing on the more flexible general revenue fund. Conversely, the public schools and junior colleges have less flexibility. They are at a disadvantage politically because if raises are desired for their faculties the legislature must approve changes in the basic state aid formulas. These changes in formula would, of course, have to apply to all institutions at that level in the state. These statewide formula changes invariably entail considerable amounts of money which must be raised by increasing taxes. Very few legislators are anxious these days to sponsor legislation calling either for new or increased taxes.

The public school suspicion that the universities may be getting a disproportionate share of the available resources will certainly find very visible expression through the tactics and activities of the FEA. The new militancy of the teachers organization may well throw the FEA into direct competition and open conflict with the university system.

Many of the educators we spoke to who feared this as a very real possibility expressed the hope that all levels of public education in Florida would coordinate their financial requests at the pre-budgetary stage. If the educators do not take such action voluntarily, the legislature, it is feared, might well impose its will upon the state's educational leaders and mandate such budgetary coordination and joint planning. If someone has to make overall budgetary decisions, it is reasoned, it might as well be educators who have the expertise on which to base their judgments and decide what educational programs should or should not be supported.

Educators express the hope that legislation can be passed which could coordinate the financial requests of all levels of public education at the pre-budgetary stage. Veteran observers of the Florida educational scene contend that it is only a question of time when all public education from kindergarten through adult education will be coordinated. The forms such coordination will take will vary from compulsory budgetary articulation to more informal strategies of joint planning.

III. GEORGIA

The Organization of Education

The Georgia Constitution provides for a division of responsibility between policy-making boards for elementary-secondary and higher education. A State Board of Education consisting of ten members appointed by the governor for seven year terms and an elected state superintendent as its executive officer is charged constitutionally with the responsibility for public elementary and secondary education. Public higher education, including the junior colleges, is constitutionally the responsibility of the Board of Regents which operates the University System of Georgia. The Board of Regents appoints the Chancellor who serves as the chief executive officer of the University System. The governor also appoints the fifteen members of the Board of Regents for seven year terms. All publicly supported education in Georgia is under the purview of one of these two boards. A third state educational agency, the Georgia Educational Improvement Council (GEIC) which was established in 1964 to serve as a liaison agency between the State Board of Education and the Board of Regents is of special interest to us and will be discussed in some detail.

Relationships between the State Board of Education and the University System

Until relatively recently there was much criticism to the effect that there was insufficient communication between the levels of education in Georgia. This lack of adequate communication and articulation of programs between the State Board and the University System was highlighted in the recent report of the Governor's Commission to Improve Education. This commission, organized in 1963 by former Governor Carl Sanders, was asked to project Georgia's future educational needs. The commission spent six months studying all levels of education in Georgia and issued its report late in 1963. The governor's mandate to the commission was to give primary attention to the development of a broad, comprehensive master plan for the improvement of education at all levels in Georgia. The governor and other Georgians were disturbed by the fact that at this time Georgia ranked 50th among the states in retaining high school age youngsters in school, 47th in percentage of its population that had completed the elementary grades, and 42nd in median school years completed by its citizens. Of particular concern to education-minded Georgians was the additional fact that in 1963 the percentage of Georgia's college age youth who attended college was only slightly more than half of the national average.

These distressing statistics compelled the governor's commission to stress rapid development of Georgia's educational system at all levels. The commission emphasized that it was particularly important for both the State Board of Education and the Board of Regents of the University System to be well staffed to engage in long term planning. The commission's report stated specifically that "the most important single prerequisite for educational improvement in Georgia is effective long-range planning."

The Georgia Education Improvement Council (GEIC)

The Georgia legislature in 1964 created the GEIC in response to the report submitted by the commission. The commission was impressed with the many areas in which the activities of the State Board and Regents were parallel or overlapping. Inter-related areas of common concern such as teacher education, college admissions policies, curricula coordination between the high schools and colleges, articulation of junior colleges and area vocational technical schools, and joint utilization of educational television were cited. The commission stated in its report:

The nature of the functions of the two statewide boards of education requires close cooperation and coordination. To achieve this, formal working relationships between the two boards should be established. The research and long-range planning units recommended should work together on problems which involve both boards. Joint committees and councils of the two boards should also be provided and the boards themselves should meet jointly on matters of common concern.

The commission emphasized the assistance required by the governor and the legislature in evaluating educational needs and formulating long-range plans. The commission thus recommended that:

The Governor and General Assembly establish a continuing agency representative of the two boards, the General Assembly and the general public to study the constantly changing long-range educational needs in Georgia and to assist in evaluating and recommending to the Governor, the General Assembly and other appropriate agencies plans and proposals for meeting them.

The GEIC is a unique state agency. It has no operating responsibilities or functions other than identifying and studying problem areas. The GEIC provides a valuable forum for representatives of all of the state's educational interests. It represents the Governor, the General Assembly, the State Board of Education, the Board of Regents, and the Georgia citizenry. The GEIC consists of ten appointed and six *ex officio* members. The governor appoints six members for staggered four year terms. The lieutenant governor and speaker of the House of Representatives appoint two senators and two representatives respectively. The six *ex officio* members are the State Superintendent of Schools, the Chairman of the State Board of Education, the Chancellor of the University System, the Chairman of the Board of Regents of the University System, the Chairman of the Senate Education Committee, and the Chairman of the House of Representatives Education Committee.

Since its inception on July 1, 1964 the GEIC has had mixed success in fulfilling its statutory mandate. The GEIC has struggled with some success to carve out a unique role for itself despite the debilitating fact that it has no authority to act. It is literally squeezed in the middle without any explicit independent decision-making power between two established state educational boards. Its very existence as a mechanism for joint study and planning is predicated upon continuous cooperation and support from the State Board and the Regents.

Supporters of the GEIC contend that its existence can be justified merely by the fact that under the council's auspices the state superintendent and Chancellor of the University System and key members of their staffs hold monthly luncheon meetings to discuss educational matters of mutual interest. In the past there had been virtually no communication between the two education boards in Georgia and regular meetings under the aegis of the GEIC represented progress. One particularly valuable by-product of these meetings has been more regularized communication between the State Education Department's Director of Vocational Education and the Regents' Director of Junior Colleges. The lack of coordination between the State Board and the Regents and their duplication of efforts in the area of vocational and technical education have been particularly sensitive and persistent issues for the legislature and governor. The GEIC, its adherents note, has also sponsored interlevel legislative seminars on educational problems, published modest but useful fact sheets, undertaken a number of studies, and in general served as a useful catalytic agent in promoting Georgia education at all levels.

More than a few observers, however, have much less glowing and sanguine estimates of the effectiveness and future role of the GEIC. They feel that the GEIC is in a powerless position with little authority, no reputation, and limited financial and staff resources. It is pointed out that the GEIC's first budget was less than the funds allocated to the University of Georgia's own Institute of Higher Education. The GEIC leadership, contend the critics, cannot afford to be dynamic or aggressive. Both the Regents and the State Board are much more powerful and entrenched agencies, and a weak fledgling like the GEIC cannot afford to offend either of the established state education boards. The studies carried out by the GEIC are "innocuous" in the estimation of some critics. The GEIC, as structured, "simply cannot be expected to do much."

The GEIC members are supportive of their organization but are puzzled about what their responsibilities are supposed to be since they are powerless to make decisions. The legislators derive prestige from their membership on the GEIC and gain political currency by being associated very visibly with a statewide educational agency. It is contended that even the legislators who are members of the GEIC, however, turn to the State Board and Regents for leadership.

Most interviewees felt that the greatest weakness of the GEIC was its annual vulnerability to the legislative appropriations process. As a tiny agency with an annual appropriation of approximately $100,000, the GEIC literally has to fight for its very survival in the legislative arena, and constantly is in a very precarious position.

The GEIC, in sum, is an agency with great potential but its future success is anything but assured.

Relationships between the State Board and the Board of Regents

The current state superintendent and chancellor have been in their positions for a relatively short period of time. Although the GEIC certainly facilitates communication, interviewees agreed that both executives were committed to cooperating with each other and that close liaison would exist even without the good offices of the new agency. The GEIC was actually in existence earlier than the incumbencies of the present superintendent and chancellor and in fact was not notably successful in getting their predecessors to work together. The historical pattern of virtually no communication and cooperation between the State Board and the Regents has been reversed by the two new top staff men in both systems. Neither the state superintendent, who took office in January, 1966, nor the chancellor, who assumed his position in March, 1966, have historical axes to grind and both are committed to the need for close working relationships.

The traditional split between the two boards is dramatized most cogently by the historical development of the community colleges and area vocational and technical schools in Georgia. Some thirty years ago the two boards began moving in divergent directions with vocational-technical schools evolving from agricultural schools under the aegis of the State Board and the junior colleges developing as entirely separate institutions under the jurisdiction of the Regents and the University System. There was virtually no communication or coordination between the two boards as somewhat duplicative and totally separate junior college and vocational and technical school programs developed. Persistent legislative concern about this overlap has already been mentioned. Recent efforts by the GEIC to establish closer coordination and have the director of junior colleges for the University System and representatives of the Education Department sit down and discuss overlapping offerings and facilities have been strongly supported by the chancellor and superintendent.

Despite recent progress, there admittedly is the need for even closer coordination between the State Board and the Regents, particularly in articulating the post high school programs of the junior colleges and the area vocational-technical schools. As one budget officer commented, "some conflict is inevitable between the levels" because of the the way in which programs are funded with "neither side giving to the other."

Historically, a statewide network of area vocational-technical schools predated the development of a master plan for junior colleges. The decision to blanket the state with these area institutions was made more than a decade ago and has been implemented already. No new area vocational-technical schools are needed although some expansion of existing plant facilities is necessary. The junior college master plan for the state was adopted only a few years ago. Future junior college expansion and programs will thus be added to an established statewide network of some 28 area vocational-technical schools.

A number of high ranking officials representing both the Regents and the State Board commented that if the state were to have the opportunity to replan its educational structure they would not recommend the fragmentation that now exists and might opt for truly comprehensive junior college programs. However unwise this rather haphazard planning was, all interviewed recognized that it was too late to relive history and a paramount goal of all educators in Georgia was to make the current structure work as effectively as possible and to articulate overlapping programs in the junior colleges and area vocational-technical schools. Despite the sincere commitment of many Regents and State Board officials to cooperate, the coordination that exists, according to some sources, was superficial and the staffs of the respective boards "still go their own way."

In Georgia, according to several sources, there has never been the feeling that the junior colleges are truly comprehensive institutions or continuations of high school. The Georgia junior colleges, some say, are heavily academically oriented and according to one Education Department official "vocational training is not considered worthy of a college label."

Education Department officials and others primarily concerned with the elementary and secondary schools were apprehensive when asked about the possibility of merging the area vocational-technical schools and junior colleges. They feared that vocational education would inevitably be subordinated to academic subjects and emasculated by the academically oriented staff of the Regents. The chancellor and other top administrators in the University System were, they said, "excellent people" but were not "occupationally oriented" in terms of their educational philosophy. The junior college presidents, for their part, were often preoccupied with their aspirations to make their institutions more prestigious four year colleges and ultimately universities. The junior college presidents thus were terribly concerned about their institution's accreditation status and the number of advanced degrees held by their faculty. With these almost irresistible forces at play it is contended that vocational education would be at a marked disadvantage if the area schools were integrated with the junior colleges under the Regents and the University System. It is readily apparent in Georgia that spokesmen for higher education differ from spokesmen for the public schools in their views on both vocational education and educational philosophy.

Some basic structural or control factors as well as philosophical issues impede the development of closer relationships between the area vocational-technical schools and the junior colleges. The area schools are mainly centrally controlled by the State Board. Some 90% of the faculty salaries in the institutions are paid by the state and the curriculum is largely mandated by state officials. Almost 50% of the budget of area schools is funded through various federal vocational aid programs which are processed and administered centrally in the Education Department. Although the State Board reportedly approved the creation of a statewide system of area vocational-technical schools a few months before the passage of the National Defense Education Act in 1958, there is little questioning the fact that the major impetus for the area school program in Georgia came from the NDEA provisions for support of technical education.

The area vocational-technical schools are, unlike the junior colleges, closely linked to the local county in which they are situated. The locality provides the site for the institutions, most of which are operated under the control of county boards of education. With a few exceptions, the directors of the state's area schools must report to the local county superintendent of schools. Only five directors of the state's nearly thirty area schools have their own boards. Control of the area schools is thus shared between the local boards of education and the State Board. The latter through its Division of Vocational Education in the State Department is responsible for overall supervision and coordination of the area schools while operational responsibility is delegated to local authorities.

The justifiable concern over duplication of facilities and programs in post high school education is exacerbated by the fear that Georgia may not be preparing adequate numbers of skilled workers to attract industry in the coming decades. Throughout the state and particularly in the Atlanta region there is a concerted effort being made to lure the new industries of the technological age into Georgia. The future economic viability of the state is in no small way contingent upon the success of these efforts. These industries require technically skilled manpower at both the semi-skilled and sub-professional job levels. There is apprehension that the area vocational-technical schools will not be able to train enough highly skilled technical workers for these sophisticated industries. Many believe that better students might be recruited into technical fields if the junior colleges were truly comprehensive and less academic.

Budget Preparation and Presentation

The State Budget Bureau legally is responsible for approving all expenditures for public education. The bureau was created in 1960 by the legislature. The governor is the *ex officio* director of the budget and appoints a state budget officer to direct the bureau. As we shall see, however, this authority is exercised quite differently for the State Board and the Regents. There is no earmarking of state funds for education in Georgia and revenues are derived from the general treasury. According to Budget Bureau officials, there is active participation in the budgetary process by both levels of education which continuously need increased financial support from the state. There is no overt fiscal competition between the levels although the State Board and the Regents and their respective staffs are vigorously engaged in the endless quest for additional resources. Neither level customarily refers publicly to the other level's budget and the ever escalating demands are not posed in a competitive context according to State Budget Bureau officials and others interviewed.

The elementary and secondary school budgets are prepared and assembled by the State Education Department. The Superintendent of Public Instruction has this legal responsibility. The Department's Financial Services Division customarily works closely with the Georgia Education Association (GEA) and other education organizations in projecting the fiscal needs of the public schools. The State Budget Bureau asks the Department to prepare a budget statement for consideration by the State Board. The State Budget Bureau then reviews the State Board approved budget.

The Budget Office wields very significant influence over elementary and secondary schools because approximately 90% of the state's expenditures are allocated on the basis of a myriad of tight line-by-line items in the budget. The Budget Bureau has the power to insure that public school funds are expended according to legal requirements and also exercises conscientiously its authority to approve budgetary transfers from item to item. The State Budget Bureau purportedly reflects legislative distaste for budgetary transfers and carefully assesses new programs proposed by the Education Department prior to approving expenditures to finance them.

After the Budget Bureau makes its detailed and significant review, the public school budget is sent to the governor who in turn then submits it to the legislature. The Education Department is asked to justify the budget before appropriate committees of the General Assembly and is assisted by the GEA, the State School Boards Association, and other educationally oriented groups in its efforts to communicate educational needs in Georgia to the legislators.

Georgia's public schools are supported primarily by state funds through a Minimum Foundation Program Act. The mandated minimum effort to be contributed (called "chargeback" in Georgia) by local school systems is to increase gradually from 16% of educational expenditures covered by the state aid formula in 1965–1966 to 20% in 1969–1970. Recently, strong legislative efforts have been made, however, to freeze the local share raised predominantly through property taxation at its 1966–1967 level of 17%. Thus the state share of support of public education is over 80%, which ranks Georgia near the top among the states in percentage of state school support. Despite this, in Georgia as elsewhere throughout the country, legislators are increasingly cognizant of the political volatility of local property tax increments.

As we have already indicated, the Regents in Georgia has great autonomy. This autonomy extends to the budgetary process. Final decision-making authority on the expenditures of Georgia's junior colleges, state colleges, and universities is centralized largely in the office of the chancellor and his fiscal staff. Formerly, universities prepared their own budgets; however, legislators reacted negatively to the diverse pressures from individual institutions, and consolidated control in the office of the chancellor and the Regents' budget staff. Some spokesmen for the University of Georgia reportedly dislike this *modus operandi* and feel that the university could do better on its own in the legislature rather than being tied in with institutions that have fewer alumni in politics and "less political clout." Despite these, and some other manifestations of displeasure with the centralized financial control exercised by the Regents, most educators in Georgia indicated support for the recent consolidation of fiscal responsibility within the central office administration of the University System. Individual institutional approaches for support tended to fragment and dissipate the influence of higher education. Now disagreements between institutions are resolved internally and non-publicly by the chancellor who thus approaches the legislature as the chief spokesman for a unified, and thus more powerful, higher education fraternity. Only the chancellor and the central office staff officially lobby in Atlanta for higher education. This system of centralized budgetary and political responsibility also insulates the operating heads of the institutions from time-consuming and non-academic lobbying activities. The Regents, its supporters contend, by submitting to the governor and legislature the overall needs of the University System precludes the vagaries of political scrutiny of each institution and thus the chances for political interference in the affairs of higher education are reduced immeasurably.

Numerous commentators on the Georgia educational scene mentioned the great contrast in budgetary discretion possessed by the Regents and by the State Board. This ostensibly is a significant source of friction between the two agencies. Members of the State Board are reported to resent the tight controls placed upon them through rather rigorous State Budget Bureau monitoring of a detailed line-item budget. They compare their position with the great fiscal flexibility enjoyed by the Regents and fail to see why the State Board is not entitled to exercise similar discretionary authority. Put differently, members of the State Board would like to have, and feel that they should possess, the power, budgetary flexibility, and prestige of the Regents. It would appear that the privileged budgetary position of the Regents *vis-à-vis* the State Board is symptomatic of feelings of inferiority sensed by those associated with the public schools. The belief seems to prevail in Georgia, correctly or incorrectly, that the Regents and its University System form a more prestigious and respected body than the State Board and its Education Department. The fact, for example, that the Chancellor of the

University System is paid a higher salary than the Superintendent of Public Instruction is reportedly resented by some status-conscious public school people.

We should point out at this time that the fiscal *carte blanche* apparently enjoyed by the Regents is circumscribed by a basic formula which largely determines what state expenditures for higher education will be. The formula is predicated on a student-faculty staffing ratio and some other factors. State support is heavily contingent upon the level of the student. Freshmen and sophomores at the university and students in the junior and state colleges are considered comparably for purposes of state aid. Classes are larger in this lower division and the student-faculty ratio upon which state reimbursement is predicated is higher. Because of higher research and instructional costs and other expenses entailed in educating upper division students a smaller student-faculty reimbursement ratio is established for programs servicing juniors and seniors at the university and graduate students.

The Role of the Governor in Georgia in Respect to the Education Budgets

In addition to his authority to appoint members of the State Board and the Regents, the governor in Georgia traditionally has exercised unusual budgetary powers. Although these powers have been curtailed considerably in recent years by a more assertive legislature, as we shall discuss in the next section, the governor still exercises great fiscal initiative and influence. The governor, until the State Budget Bureau became operational only a few years ago, had virtually unlimited budgetary control, as his own budget officer. The legislature, until recently, was in essence powerless on fiscal matters. The governor controlled the appropriations process which was consonant with the state tradition of strong executive leadership. Even the creation of the State Budget Bureau has not really altered the strong executive budget pattern in Georgia because the Director of the Bureau is appointed by the governor and serves at his pleasure as the state's executive budget officer.

The Georgia Legislature and the Budgetary Process

As we have already indicated, the Georgia General Assembly is in the process of tooling itself up to play a more influential and sophisticated role in the budgetary process. The legislative committees dealing with fiscal matters, however, still do not have adequate staff assistance. Although the Appropriations Committee may spend three solid weeks conducting budgetary hearings at which department heads testify, the legislature is still not in a position to manifest the expertise required to effectively determine fiscal policy. In the words of one official, the legislature only "tinkers" with an executive budget that is imposed upon it. If the General Assembly were to play a truly influential role in setting fiscal policy, legislators would have to be involved much earlier in the preliminary stages of the budgetary process. The education committees, called the Educational Matters Committee in the Senate and the Standing Committee on Education in the House, have no fiscal powers whatsoever. A single Appropriations Committee is responsible for legislative review of all education budgets. The committee, however, is divided into two sub-committees one of which focuses on elementary and secondary school expenditures while the other concentrates on reviewing the budget of the University System.

Several factors are cited as precipitating the recent assertiveness of the legislature on budgetary matters. Georgia's political structure has been altered significantly by legislative reapportionment. The impact of the "one man, one vote" doctrine perhaps has been greater in Georgia than in other states because it has caused the demise of the state's county unit representation system through which the rural interests had for years completely dominated the legislature. Although the process of reapportioning the Georgia General Assembly still is not complete, observers note that the current crop of more "urbanized" legislators is "conscientious" and "sophisticated." The "new breed" feel that they have obligations as elected representatives of the people to become more knowledgeable about the way public funds are expended.

Private Groups and Educational Decision-Making in Georgia

The Georgia Education Association

The Georgia Education Association (GEA) is considered by most observers to be by far the most politically influential educational organization in the state. With a grass roots membership of more than 30,000 located throughout the state, the GEA represents every segment of education and must be influential through the sheer weight of its members. The Association's nine departments represent elementary and secondary school teachers and principals, curriculum specialists, persons in higher education, librarians, counselors, and administrators. Officials of the GEA include representatives from their Department of Higher Education on all state committees in each of the GEA's ten geographic regions. The GEA also asks the University System and the State Department to participate on its committees on an *ex officio* basis. The Association's legislative program includes statements of support for budgetary requests made by the University System. This purportedly reflects the GEA's concern for the whole spectrum of education from kindergarten through graduate school.

The GEA, like its counterparts in a growing number of states, is becoming more controversial. Some critics of the Association resent its militant tactics and believe that the legislators are influenced more by Education Department officials. The GEA, it is contended, like labor unions has "to beat its drums constantly to survive" and thus employs pressure tactics which frequently annoy legislators. One legislator commented that it was not uncommon to have the GEA referred to on the floor of the General Assembly as the "largest union in Georgia."

Although the teachers union has not been very active yet in Georgia and is not in any way, at this time, a threat or spur to the GEA, there are manifestations of unrest and rising militancy appearing, particularly among younger teachers. These young teachers want the Association to stress raising beginning salaries so that they can remain in the classroom and not be compelled, for economic reasons, to leave education or become administrators. There is some feeling among these "Young Turks" that the GEA is administrator-oriented and dominated and thus focuses its efforts on salary increments for older teachers.

The GEA, despite criticisms of its operations and aggressive leadership, usually gets what it wants since it is the most influential organization of its kind in the state. In the 1967 legislative session, for example, the GEA proposal for salary increases pegged to an index scale prevailed over considerable opposition in the legislative and executive branches of government. Opponents of the Association favored across-the-board increments but the GEA was successful in its efforts and a new index plan for teacher salaries was established which permits an average salary increase of more than $1,200 per teacher for the 1967–1969 biennium.

The Georgia School Boards Association

The Georgia School Boards Association (SBA) has been in existence for only fifteen years. According to some observers, it has not been particularly effective at the state level. In recent years the SBA reportedly has been focusing its attention upon educational issues at the local level. A few critics contend that the organization is conservative and dominated by rural interests which desire to stymie implementation of the federal desegregation guidelines. Efforts by some leaders of the SBA to fight the guidelines are purported to embarrass the Education Department which allegedly is taking a more moderate position on civil rights issues.

The SBA cooperates closely with the GEA and the organizations never openly oppose each other. The rising teacher militancy which in other states has caused the estrangement of teachers associations from their traditional organizational alliances with school boards and administrators groups is not yet present in Georgia. The leadership of the GEA and the SBA is aware of what is happening in other states and is "working hard" to maintain close working relationships to forestall the "germination of the seeds of teacher unionism" in Georgia.

Public school administrators

The public school administrators in Georgia are organizationally fragmented. Elementary and secondary school principals are organized as separate departments of the GEA. The Georgia Association of School Administrators is likewise structured as a department within the GEA framework and is described by one of its former officers as being "weak" and "feeble." Apparently the only administrators group with even a modicum of independent strength is the organization of Chief School Officers consisting of the superintendents of Georgia's 196 school districts. This organization which works closely with the Education Department, however, is handicapped by its lack of full time staff, inadequate resources, and a nebulous organizational structure. There is no permanent executive secretary and a practicing superintendent serves as a part time legislative representative. It may appear that school superintendents have very limited political influence in Georgia because of their apparent organizational weaknesses, but several atypical factors have to be borne in mind. In essence, the administrators may not need a powerful organization of their own because of the influence they exercise within the GEA and the GSBA.

Of even greater significance, however, is the fact that as of the 1964–1965 school year, 134 of Georgia's 196 school superintendents were elected by registered voters in their counties. In these counties, which for the most part are in rural sections, the superintendent as an elected official is usually part of the "court house clique" that controls the county politically and determines the makeup of the Grand Jury which in turn appoints members of the county board of education. In 1964–1965, 551 or almost 50% of Georgia's 1,140 school board members were appointed by Grand Juries.

Thus in Georgia an anomalous political structure enables superintendents in 104 school systems to play a major role in the selection of the board members whom they ostensibly will be responsible to. This situation obviously gives the chief school officers in these counties unusual influence *vis-à-vis* their boards of education. These administrators are obviously practicing politicians in every sense of the word and must behave accordingly. State certification procedures and regional accreditation, however, do impose some restraints on eligibility for service as county superintendents. A masters degree, for example, is required for state certification as a county superintendent. In some of the poorer rural areas, however, it is difficult to find qualified candidates to run for county superintendent. Most of the educational leaders interviewed agreed that making these chief administrators appointive officials would improve the caliber of educational leadership in the state immeasurably and enhance the status of their statewide organization. Because of the political nature of their offices, the elected superintendents in many counties are infinitely more conservative and less responsive to change than their school boards. This can be seen in their attitudes toward civil rights problems and other educationally related issues. Many observers believe that the *sine qua non* of meaningful educational improvement and reform in Georgia is predicated upon changing the selection patterns of local education officials. It is apparent, however, that many of Georgia's school administrators have unique political leverage.

Private groups and higher education

As we have suggested, the centralized authority and great influence of the Chancellor and the Regents obviates the need for private organizations to become heavily involved in mustering support for higher education. The concentration of budgetary authority vested in the office of the University System's Treasurer eliminates institutional competition and minimizes alumni politicking.

No private groups in the state have been noticeably active in focusing upon education at the 13th and 14th grade levels and the state-level political activity of private educational institutions appears to be nil.

The Georgia Education Coordinating Committee

The Georgia Education Coordinating Committee was organized some five years ago by the School Boards Association in an effort to coordinate the activities and legislative programs of the state's major educational interest groups. Representatives of the School Boards Association, the GEA, the State Board, the University System, the PTA, and two administrators organizations, as well as the Dean of the University of Georgia's School of

Education usually meet quarterly to discuss educational matters of common concern. During a legislative year the committee may meet as frequently as is necessary. Although attempts are made to develop a consensus among the constituent organizations, the committee is voluntary and loosely knit and no group is bound by its decisions unless the organization's Board of Directors concurs.

The committee has no permanent staff or resources of its own. It carries on no independent research and issues no publications. The committee simply provides a forum at which the state's educational leaders can get together and talk things through. Although the constituent organizations maintain their independence not to go along with committee proposals, the meetings at least provide an opportunity for the leadership of the respective groups to learn how others feel and think about current issues. In the past, efforts to bring the State Board and Regents together were unsuccessful and the committee has served a vital function in providing a mechanism for enabling the two boards to meet regularly. The committee focuses on public school matters but the budget of the University System as well as the budget of the State Board is discussed and reacted to by the committee prior to legislative sessions. These meetings reportedly reflect the cooperation of the two levels of education in Georgia and the concerted efforts made to avoid competition for resources.

Despite the efforts made by the committee to coordinate the activities of Georgia's educational organizations, each interest group, according to several commentators, frequently continues "to paddle its own canoe." Several public school spokesmen expressed annoyance that a representative of the Regents had not appeared at a recent committee meeting and that no explanation for the absence had been given. Supporters of the committee's work, while confessing its weaknesses, stated that it would serve a valuable purpose if it did nothing but bring the various groups together. These advocates contend that the committee forges an effective coalition for supporting major educational proposals by establishing legislative priorities on which its constituent organizations can agree. Some of the committee's supporters, while avowing that much is accomplished because Georgia's educational organizations "stay tied up in a bundle," admit that the coalition can be greatly strengthened. Many of the "loosely knit and loosely committed" committee's most ardent supporters would like to see it more formally organized, staffed with permanent personnel, and generously funded.

Other observers of the Georgia educational scene were quite critical of the committee's efforts and regarded it as an ineffectual group. One prominent official in the Education Department had "only heard" of its activities. Other critics commented that they had not seen any "concrete results" and that the committee was impotent to prevent the state's educational organizations from fragmenting and going their own way. The committee allegedly almost fell apart recently when the State Education Department reportedly did not coordinate its legislative activities with other groups and left some organizations "out on the political limb" when a budgetary change was made unexpectedly. One legislator assessed the committee as being "overrated" and "overplayed." He complained that the committee is valuable only as a "sounding board," which never lines up legislative sponsors for its proposals and is never concrete enough in its recommendations. Legislators, according to this source, do not actively solicit advice from the committee on educational legislation nor do they seek its endorsement for their proposals.

The activities of the committee tend to be similar to the work of the Georgia Education Improvement Council (GEIC) and questions were posed as to whether the two groups duplicated efforts. If the committee had been successful in coordinating the activities of the educational organizations why was it necessary to establish the GEIC? The GEIC, incidentally, is an *ex officio* member of the committee and its executive director attends meetings. The GEIC provides a full time staff which works on coordination throughout the year and not on an irregular, *ad hoc* basis as the committee does. There is no conflict or duplication because the committee meets infrequently and the chancellor, for example, who regularly attends GEIC sessions, participates infrequently in committee meetings, usually only at times when budgets are discussed.

Impressions and Projections

There appears to be in Georgia a great deal of cooperation between the levels of education. Instrumentalities such as the Georgia Education Improvement Council and the Georgia Education Coordinating Committee provide channels through which constant dialogue occurs between the leadership of the public schools and higher education. Although some interviewees did speculate about the eventuality of the State Board and Regents merging into a single "superboard," this prospect seems very remote for the foreseeable future. Representatives of both existing boards oppose the creation of a "superboard" which would coordinate all publicly supported education in the state. They contend vigorously that both boards have more than enough to do in their respective spheres and believe that contemporary educational problems are far too complex and varied for a single body to assume overall responsibility effectively.

Despite the high degree of cooperation that exists and the sincere efforts that are being made to present a unified front, it is impossible even in Georgia to avert aspects of competition completely. The recent increases in the University System's budget, for example, were described as "phenomenal" and "fantastic" by some educators. Some public school leaders, however, reportedly were somewhat concerned and uneasy about the unprecedented successes of the University System which in the last legislative session, unlike the State Board, received all the fiscal support it requested.

Much of the credit for the renaissance in higher education in Georgia was attributed to the dynamic and effective leadership of the recently appointed Chancellor of the University System. Before his arrival in Atlanta, the Regents allegedly went to the legislature "hat in hand" with very minimal budgetary requests. The public schools reportedly were much more effective politically and fared better financially.

The recent growth in the political influence of the highly centralized University System was compared to the rather diffuse public school system in Georgia. The Regents possess an advantage in having a "tight ship" which can be steered independently from the political constraints that influence the public schools. The public schools of Georgia with strong local control norms are under diverse and numerous pressures and structurally are inextricably woven into the state's political fabric. It is difficult for the State Board or its professional staff to unify a vague and lumbering structure in which 197 school districts have much autonomy. Many commentators believe that chances for effective state leadership and coordination are vitiated by the state's basic educational structure. The chief state school officer, they point out, as an elected official is always running for office and is reluctant to antagonize any segment of voters by exercising aggressive leadership. The Education Department, it is felt, thus is reluctant to impose standards or withhold funds from recalcitrant local districts that do not adhere to state prescribed guidelines. It is contended by those who want the chief state school officer's position to become appointive that many very able prospective candidates for the job are reluctant to run for political office on a partisan basis. The rural interests in the state want to maintain an elected chief state school officer and despite persistent talk about changing the selection process, it appears unlikely that such a change will occur in the near future.

Although higher education is undeniably making significant strides in Georgia, it still has a long way to go and is relatively underfinanced. Officials of the University System note that in Georgia only 26% of the college age population is in school as compared to the national average of 47%. In the fall of 1966, there were some 60,000 students enrolled in the University System. According to national norms, there should have been 100,000. Although expenditures for higher education have tripled in ten years, many Georgians believe that the state's spending for this purpose will have to climb at an even faster rate to serve the increasing numbers of youth who want a college education. Georgia is not a wealthy state. There is particular concern that there are not adequate opportunities for comparatively cheap public higher education for the state's sizeable numbers of low income Negroes and whites. It thus seems reasonable to predict that despite the recent dramatic increments, expenditures for higher education will continue to soar in the future.

Educators at all levels at the time of our visit to Atlanta were particularly apprehensive about a Georgia County Commissioners' recommendation that the state assume full responsibility for financing the public schools. This proposal would earmark all property taxes to support local governments other than school districts. It concerns educators because the University System has two sources of revenue, student fees and state grants. The public schools, of course, are currently supported by the property tax as well as state aid. It is feared that if the public schools were to lose their access to the property tax, the state would have to take up the financial slack from the same general revenue funds which support higher education. The State Board and the Education Department actively opposed the tax recommendations of the County Commissioners for several reasons: not only because they fear erosion of local control if the state alone were to support the public schools, but also because of their concern that such a change in taxing patterns might put the State Board on a collision course in competing with the increasingly influential University System for the same sources of revenue.

IV. ILLINOIS

At present, there is no open conflict between elementary-secondary and higher education in Illinois but the potential for competition for the limited resources for educational purposes is developing rapidly and conflict between the levels of education is certain to assert itself soon.

The Organization of Education

The government of elementary-secondary education

The government of elementary-secondary education in Illinois appeared to be in a state of transition prior to the 1967 session of the General Assembly. This Assembly addressed itself to correcting some of the educational decision-making procedures in Illinois.

The traditional decision-making system for elementary-secondary education is composed of the legislature, the governor's office, the Office of Public Instruction, the professional education organizations such as the Illinois Education Association (IEA) and the Illinois School Boards Association (ISBA), the continuing and *ad hoc* pressure groups related to education such as the Illinois Federation of Taxpayers, and the School Problems Commission (SPC). The Office of Public Instruction is headed by a superintendent who is elected state-wide on a partisan ballot. Except for the SPC, the roles of the components are self-explanatory.

The SPC is a quasi-legislative advisory agency to the state legislature composed of five state representatives, five senators, five gubernatorial appointees, the State Superintendent of Public Instruction and the Director of Finance. It is officially responsible for studying (1) school district reorganization, (2) revision of school laws, (3) the interrelationship of state, county, and local school administration, (4) the method of acquiring adequate school revenue, and (5) any problem that may affect the general welfare of the schools. In the past, the SPC has served as the originator of most major school legislation. Its recommendations to the General Assembly have been non-controversial and usually unanimous because of a deep commitment on the part of its members to achieve internal cohesion.

The SPC is the only agency of its type in the United States. Its uniqueness is due partly to the fact that Illinois is one of two states without a state board of education at the elementary-secondary level. For this reason, the SPC has been performing many functions usually reserved for a state board, such as conducting preliminary research for legislation and recommending legislation to the General Assembly.

The pattern of education decision-making prior to the 1967 session of the legislature was predetermined and unalterable. The SPC decided what education bills would be recommended to the legislature and in an effort to minimize conflict and controversy certain types of problems were deliberately avoided. Consequently, educators knew how the SPC would react to each type of bill and the ultimate decision was predictable. This fixed educational decision-making pattern provided for the solution of education problems in an atmosphere free of competition in the political arena at the expense of policy alternatives and financial goals.

The existence of the SPC as the predominant component of the elementary-secondary decision-making system was seriously threatened during the last session of the legislature when the Governor's Task Force Commission recommended that (1) a state board of education with jurisdiction over elementary and secondary education be created and (2) the state board appoint the state superintendent of public instruction. The creation of these offices would eliminate the need for the SPC. These recommendations were killed in the legislature.

At least seven commissions since 1907 have recommended a state board of education and an appointive superintendent for administering state-wide elementary-secondary education. They have consistently pointed out the need for centralized responsibility, long-range planning, professional expertise in a nonpartisan setting, and continuity and efficiency in the educational operations. The legislature has defeated all such proposals. But even against these odds the Governor's Task Force made its proposal and perceived it to be of the highest priority, primarily as a necessary first step through which many of the other Task Force recommendations could be implemented. The crucial stumbling block in the recommendation for an appointive board was its method of selecting members—whether they should be gubernatorially appointed, elected, or a combination of the two. A compromise bill proposed by SPC was introduced in the senate which called for a fifteen-member state board, eight elected from eight "educational districts," five appointed by the Governor, and two *ex officio* members representing the two houses of the legislature.

The proposal to create educational districts introduced a politically explosive issue, and as a consequence the bill was never considered seriously by the legislature. The bill never got out of the Senate Education Committee and its companion bill was tabled in the House Appropriations Committee on the specious argument that more extensive study should be made in a proposed Constitutional Convention which never materialized. There was a vacuum of key leadership on this issue in both parties.

The realities of the present political scene indicate that any change in state-level administrative structure is years away. The incumbent educational decision-makers have acquired their positions via the current system and thus are not very critical of it. In fact, they question any proposal to upset the *status quo*. The component of the educational decision-making system most threatened by a state board or appointive superintendent would be the Office of Public Instruction, which has been responsible for most of the functions commonly assigned to a state board. This office has been constantly surrounded by a high degree of partisan politics but still has managed exceptional continuity and substantial leadership.

Pressures for a state board and appointive superintendent have not been extreme. Legislators have felt no serious mandate from the people for change, and have been quite well satisfied with the educational leadership of the superintendent and the SPC.

Because there is no state board in Illinois, the governor, state superintendent of public instruction, and interest groups play a somewhat different role in educational decision-making than they do in other states.

The governor and the SPC in Illinois have traditionally been interdependent. The governor, by virtue of his responsibility to appoint six members of the 17-member SPC, his control over state finances, and his veto power could exercise a measure of control over SPC. On the other hand, he depended on the SPC for advice as to the identity and political implications of educational problems.

The role of the superintendent of public instruction has taken on new significance since the increased involvement of the federal government in education. As the state official responsible for the distribution of funds, his political influence, which was considerable before, has been enhanced. He still remains chief adviser to the SPC which takes credit for any educational recommendations he may make. Since he cannot make a public reputation as an education expert, he is forced to do so as a partisan politician. The partisan political and professional roles of the superintendent are incompatible. The separation of the office from partisan politics might provide the superintendent with the opportunity to assert true leadership in educational decision-making.

It was mentioned earlier in this report that there has been a pattern of high predictability in Illinois educational decision-making. In the past, the goals of private educational interest groups have been sacrificed in order to preserve this pattern of predictable decision-making. Evidence of this is the fact that today Illinois ranks forty-eighth among the states in percentage of school revenue supplied by the state. Only about twenty-three percent of the total school revenue comes from the state.

Present evidence is that professional educators still consider the safety of high predictability to be desirable. They would rather be sure of some resources than take a chance of not getting anything. The Illinois Education Association (IEA) decides what it can get from the legislature then tempers its demands accordingly. There is evidence also to indicate that the Illinois School Boards Association (ISBA) is satisfied with the present pattern of educational decision-making.

Those vigorously seeking a new pattern of educational decision-making, except for the Illinois Federation of Teachers, are not the professional educators. A small group of liberal legislators seem to be leading this movement. These legislators have criticized the SPC, the IEA and other professional groups for not forming a coalition of lay and professional education organizations, patterned after the New York State Educational Conference Board, to compete for a larger share of the state's resources for elementary-secondary education.

It is safe to predict that the IEA, ISBA, IASA (Illinois Association of School Administrators), and the County Superintendents Association will eventually form a coalition. A group with such a diversified membership will provide the instrument needed for substituting educational goals for political harmony in educational decision-making.

Under the existing organization, the needs of lower education are weakly represented. Lack of organized government for elementary-secondary education makes it more difficult to bring an educational problem to focus in Illinois compared with states with a strong state board. Education in Illinois takes place under considerable political tension because of the elected partisan state superintendent and in spite of the basically non-partisan SPC.

The government of higher education

The system of higher education in Illinois is composed of five separate "systems," each assigned a somewhat different role. The activities of these systems are tempered by the Illinois Board of Higher Education. This board was created in 1961 to provide a permanent coordinating and planning agency for the entire higher education structure. One of its continuing functions is the development of a statewide master plan for higher education.

The board determines the roles of the various sub-systems, approves new programs, and screens all budgets before they are submitted to the legislature. It has sixteen members, ten appointed by the governor plus the five presidents of the sub-system boards and the superintendent of public instruction.

One component of the system is the University of Illinois Board of Trustees. The university trustees are responsible for governing the main campus at Urbana, the Chicago Circle campus and the medical center in Chicago. The board's functions include providing facilities, hiring faculties and administrators, fixing tuition rates and the like. Of the five systems, the University of Illinois Board is the only one which is chosen by the voters, with nine members elected on a statewide basis and the governor and superintendent serving *ex officio*.

The Southern Illinois University Board of Trustees has essentially the same authority as the University of Illinois Board. Seven trustees are appointed by the governor with the superintendent as an eighth member.

The third component of the higher education system in Illinois is the Board of Governors, State Colleges and Universities. This eleven member board governs four former teachers colleges now offering broader programs. Nine members are appointed by the governor and the superintendent of public instruction and state finance director also serve on the board. Growth has been phenomenal in the schools governed by this board, which now has a larger enrollment under its jurisdiction than any of the other boards.

The Illinois Junior College Board, while responsible for development of the fast growing junior college system, is not exactly a governing board. It was formed in 1965 to perform essentially the same planning and coordinating functions for the junior colleges that the Board of Higher Education does for the whole system. It approves new junior college districts, sets standards, and allots the 75% of the costs of new construction which will be paid by the state. The board consists of eight appointed members and the superintendent. Individual junior college districts are managed by seven member boards, chosen like local school boards and with similar taxing and governing powers. In Chicago, the board is appointed by the mayor; elsewhere board members are elected. There are presently twenty-seven districts in operation.

In 1967, the Board of Regents, which governs Illinois State University and Northern Illinois University, was created. It consists of nine members appointed by the governor and the state superintendent. The rationale cited for the creation of this board is that its two universities have the greatest potential for developing doctoral programs designed to prepare much needed college professors.

Issues in Illinois Educational Politics

In Illinois there appears to be a large number of controversial issues within the two levels of education, but few meaningful conflicts seem to develop between levels. The controversy over an appointive superintendent and a state board of education in the elementary-secondary level was basically an intralevel problem. At the higher education level, the problems were also on an intralevel scale. There are issues which do transcend both levels but they are not yet of major consequence. There is at present little open conflict between education levels for the state's scarce resources.

Master Plan for higher education—Phase II

Even though the Master Plan-Phase II created more of an intralevel than an interlevel controversy, its very existence and timing caused competition between educational levels for favorable consideration in the legislature. Phase II dealt with the reorganization of higher education as described in the section on the government of higher education. It also proposed four new residential colleges located in the Chicago metropolitan area and in Springfield. These new colleges were primarily for junior college transfer students and were to offer programs for junior, senior, and first-year graduate students only. The purpose was to strengthen the role of the junior college and lessen the impact of these new schools on non-public colleges in the area. Phase II evoked considerable controversy, but the controversy remained within the realm of higher education. The non-public schools reacted violently to the establishment of these colleges and a heated argument broke out over which board would have authority over the new colleges.

The implementation of Phase II of the Master Plan for higher education showed clearly that higher education enjoys a preferred position in the eyes of the legislature and the governor, due probably to the spirit of the times. There is no question that the demands for higher education are popular and pressing, but it is also evident that the demands of higher education are much better articulated than those of elementary-secondary. Both elementary-secondary and higher education brought important legislation before the 1967 session of the legislature. The Task Force recommendations and the Phase II recommendations hit the legislators at about the same time prior to the 1967 session with a budget request of one billion dollars each. The appropriation for higher education was pared by only three percent. However, elementary-secondary education received only half of its budget request.

The legislative package emanating from the Governor's Task

Force was never a serious threat to Phase II of the Master Plan and the other higher education bills before the 1967 session. The recommendations of the Task Force did not have the unified support of the professional leaders or the education committees before they reached the legislature. Higher education did have such support. It is conceivable that the Task Force recommendations simply did not strengthen elementary-secondary education enough to warrant a change in its political status *vis-à-vis* higher education.

The part played by the governor also influenced the legislators favorably toward higher education in the 1967 session. Phase II of the Master Plan was admittedly a top gubernatorial priority. This concern for the Master Plan, supported by the governor, crowded out most lower education issues, and particularly affected the legislative response of the 1967 session of the General Assembly to the Task Force recommendations.

Elementary-secondary education was hurt by higher education during the 1967 session of the legislature. The two levels of education were forced into competition which is certain to become overt in the very near future because elementary-secondary education cannot continue to emerge second best.

Education in the thirteenth and fourteenth grades

As a result of Phase I of the Master Plan for higher education, the 1965 General Assembly approved a Public Junior College Act. The act moved the junior colleges into higher education. It removed the junior colleges from the supervision of the state superintendent of public instruction and placed them under the authority of a State Junior College Board. This reorganization had two advantages: (1) it provided an increase in operating aid and (2) it made available state construction grants up to seventy-five percent of construction costs. These two inducements plus local interest generated by the state-wide discussions of the Master Plan provided a speedy reorganization of existing colleges and prompt creation of new junior college districts. The only junior college district that did not respond immediately to the incentives was in Chicago.

As an institution governed by the elementary-secondary educational system in Chicago, the City Junior College experienced rapid growth. Support for the City Junior College was appropriated by the Chicago Board of Education at a rate of eight million dollars annually. Many who opposed state control of the junior college in Chicago regard it as a neighborhood institution attuned to the special needs and problems of a locale. But those in favor of state control pointed out that because of the pupil population boom expected in the next decade, local boards will have enough challenge just to meet elementary-secondary needs.

The Superintendent of the Chicago Schools was opposed to state control of the City Junior College for various reasons which the Board of Higher Education considered specious. After a period of heated argument, the Chicago Board of Education overruled the superintendent and relinquished control of the junior colleges to the state.

Vocational-technical education

Another aspect of the interlevel relationship of thirteenth and fourteenth grade education in Illinois is the matter of vocational-technical training. The Governor's Task Force recommended that the Board of Vocational Education and Rehabilitation which meets as two separate boards be reconstituted as one board, called the State Board of Occupational Resource Development, to operate under a proposed State Board of Education (elementary-secondary). Since the State Board of Education was non-existent, the Office of the Superintendent formulated a legislative package designed to amend all arrangements for vocational education, transfer the Board of Vocational Education to the Office of Public Instruction, and establish a vocational education advisory board. This legislation was tabled in the Senate Education Committee.

In its recommendation to place vocational education under the newly proposed State Board of Education, the Task Force was, in a sense, ignoring the role of the junior colleges in vocational education, the Task Force studies indicate that occupational education will be a significant part of elementary and secondary programs for a long time.

Elementary-secondary state aid

Elementary-secondary education has not fared well in its struggle for adequate funds to improve the quality of education in Illinois. Efforts to have the state aid formula changed have invariably resulted in political hassles in the legislature. The only real solution to the financial problems of both levels of education in Illinois is fiscal reform. When the Task Force suggested bold fiscal changes in the form of a personal and corporate income tax as the best means by which to obtain the needed school revenue, it was rebuked by political and other interests as being neither politically expedient or necessary and not within the province of the Task Force study.

The Governor's Task Force proposed a foundation program of state aid with a minimum figure of $600 compared with the $335 figure in existence at the time. The legislature countered with a bill providing a $400 foundation rate. This figure was accepted by Republican leadership in the Office of the Superintendent of Public Instruction, the SPC, and the legislature, and endorsed by the governor. The $600 foundation figure recommended by the Task Force was considered very realistic. The actual state-wide operating costs during the previous school year averaged $540 per pupil. The national average was even higher. However, the $600 figure was not feasible for immediate legislation under the current taxing structure of the state. The $400 figure was politically expedient and satisfied the demands of the educators and conservatives in the legislature.

Elementary-secondary education cannot continue to be satisfied with the inadequate support that it receives from the state. Considering the generous support provided for higher education, it will not be long before there is overt conflict for funds between the levels of education.

The Future of Education in Illinois

Despite the fact that public higher education in Illinois is satisfactorily provided for, there is evidence that the overall outlook for education is grave and that elementary-secondary education will soon be in serious structural and financial trouble. This set of circumstances can only lead to increased interlevel competition within education. There is reason to predict that in spite of the failure of the Task Force to persuade the 1967 legislature to enact new educational decision-making patterns, there will, in the next few years, be changes in the approach to educational problems. The reasons are inherent in the facts that (1) the SPC and the partisan state superintendent can no longer speak effectively for elementary-secondary interests, (2) the increased involvement of the federal government at all levels will demand better solutions to state education problems, (3) liberal legislators will want answers to teacher welfare questions and urban problems that the present system now ignores, and (4) the state-aid formula will simply have to be changed by the legislature because local tax bases cannot support the schools.

The increasing costs of education are going to force the levels of education in Illinois to compete actively for the scarce resources of the state. It is predicted that the demands on the educational decision-making system of the future will be such that the system will not be able to tolerate domination by one component, such as higher education. There is no question that a coalition will have to be formed to insure that education assumes a cooperative, aggressive role within the overall political system. It is this type of emphasis that will be needed to prevent the overt competition between educational levels that can only be detrimental to education in Illinois.

V. INDIANA

A review of the politics of education in Indiana, and more particularly, interlevel relationships, reveals that little is happening in the state. While this comment doubtless oversimplifies the situation, Indiana seems to embody the traditional condition of educational politics in its unspoiled form. While other states are experiencing upheavals or undergoing serious self-examinations, Indiana maintains a surface, at least, of placid fragmentation and unconcern.

The Organization of Education in Indiana

The government of elementary-secondary education

The formal structure of education at the state level in Indiana centers upon an elective State Superintendent and an appointive State Board of Education. The state constitution specifies that "The General Assembly shall provide for the election, by the voters of the State, of a State Superintendent of Public Instruction, who shall hold his office for two years, and whose duties and compensation shall be prescribed by law." The office is sought on a partisan ballot. The present superintendent was a social studies teacher from Gary (a Lake County industrial town) and a vice-president of the Indiana State Teachers Association (ISTA). He won the office in a Republican "sweep" which changed party control of the lower house of the legislature and reversed relative party strength of the state's congressional delegation.

Traditionally, the state office and the ISTA have been very close, some say virtually indistinguishable. The relationship is rather weakened at present, however. The department and superintendent have provided little in the way of leadership over a long period of time, a condition that relates intimately to the general theme of our discussion. Perhaps four factors help explain this action vacuum at the top of the state system. One is the fact that the superintendent, serving a two-year term, is always running for re-election. Secondly, the close relationship with the ISTA, while it might have been a source of strength, has probably instead been an inhibiting factor on the development of leadership in the state office. Thirdly, the general political tradition of Indiana has encouraged diffusion of power. Fourthly, the superintendency has doubtless been somewhat weakened by the fact that there is in the structure a statutory board of education. While the superintendent is not without influence on the board, its very existence modifies his independence to some unknown degree.

Thus the state office appears to have had chiefly an administrative role. The Teachers Association has carried the ball on most important policy matters, and the elective independence of the superintendent has freed the governor from assuming some of the responsibility. The present governor has apparently neither been very interested in education nor particularly successful with the legislature.

The Indiana State Board of Education is an even stranger phenomenon. From 1852 to 1945 it was a rather conventional body concerned chiefly with financial matters. In the latter year the legislature divided the board into three commissions to deal, respectively, with teacher training and licensing, textbook adoption, and general, *i.e.*, residual, functions. Each commission is composed of six members appointed by the governor, plus the state superintendent *ex officio*. The superintendent serves as chairman of the commissions and makes agenda for them. While the board might meet as a whole body, apparently it does not. Perhaps the most significant feature of board structure is that a majority of the members of each commission must by law be professional educators.

The commissions seem to perform an active part in both policy-making and administration. They apparently do actually dip into the processes of accreditation and textbook adoption, handling the routine load of ordinary cases with staff help from the State Office. There is little coordination among them and most critics regard the structure as extraordinarily cumbersome.

The implications of this structure are treated in subsequent pages in connection with specific issues. They seem to be quite predictable from the structure itself; that is to say, the texture of educational politics in Indiana is very much what one would expect from this skeletal description of the formal organization.

The government of higher education

Indiana has not done badly in its support of public colleges in comparison with its neighboring states. Its appropriations as a proportion of personal income exceed those of Illinois, Michigan, Ohio, and Wisconsin, and its appropriations *per capita* exceed those of all these states except Michigan. Public higher education has thus been rather well-treated.

With minimal exceptions that will be noted below, the entire public higher educational enterprise is concentrated in the hands of four institutions: Indiana University, Purdue University, Indiana State University, and Ball State University. There is no overriding structure of higher education in Indiana. Each of the four institutions has its own independent governing board appointed by the governor. Each has established its own political base, and each relates to the legislature in a quite independent way. By all reports, both Indiana University and Purdue have been very successful with the legislature where they benefit from the support of a good number of alumni. There is some feeling of resentment among other political interests in the state, including elementary-secondary people, about the tremendous clout the universities are said to have.

Political Power in Public Education

The matter of political power in Indiana public education is in the first instance the matter of political power of the State Teachers Association. The importance of the ISTA is well-enough known that it does not require treatment at great length. It must certainly have been one of the most powerful groups of its kind in the country, perhaps one of the most successful political groups of any kind.

The ISTA has apparently benefited from, and in turn contributed to, the weakness of the formal structure of educational authority in the state. Its importance to the board and to the office has been very great; a person associated with ISTA commented that under the former superintendent, relationships "couldn't have been closer." This has meant that ISTA has generally taken the lead in developing policy positions for education and promoting them before the legislature. The group is said to have remarkable access to the assembly; the State Office, however, seems to have but little. Thus, on salaries and school finance, reorganization, accreditation, etc., the ISTA has been the force to reckon with.

As in some other states, what appears to have been a stable

political relationship among the legislature, the state education structure, and the Teachers Association is now somewhat threatened. The dimensions of the threat and the causes of it cannot be gauged with certainty. It is, in part, very subtle and perhaps, in part, temporary.

One of the factors that probably figures in the picture is the growing complexity, cost, and visibility of education as a public function. A second factor is the mounting power of the teachers' unions. (The direct threat to ISTA has doubtless helped it to ward off the appeal of the union.) Its orientation has come closer to the union perspective than that of most NEA affiliates. The ISTA is by no means oblivious to the possibility of union growth, but neither is it panicked. At present, Indiana has no professional negotiations legislation; ISTA would like to see a bill pass that would accord it exclusive recognition.

Another factor in the present situation of ISTA is its relationship to the other portions of the elementary-secondary education profession. In Indiana, the administrators and school boards associations are housed in Bloomington at the university. Relations between these groups and ISTA appear to be strained, and this strain to some extent feeds back on the university itself. Some seem to feel that the university has tried to establish domination over the elementary-secondary field by co-opting important elements of it. This arrangement spreads the efforts and influence of the elementary-secondary education groups and it is also at least a minor irritant limiting cooperation between educational levels.

Finally, the role of the ISTA has doubtless changed somewhat with the election of the present superintendent. Certainly, one of its primary strengths has been its close ties with the State Department, ties that according to several respondents are now more tenuous.

From the above discussion it is clear that the teachers' group has been the predominant influence in the entire elementary-secondary scene. If our diagnosis of the situation is correct, it also seems that the politics of the field is growing more diffuse, losing some of the coherence it formerly enjoyed.

Issues in the Relationship of Elementary-Secondary and Higher Education

Financing schools and colleges

The state's school support is conventional. It shows the financial strain one finds in all states as educational costs mount, and it certainly bears the seeds of interlevel conflict as that strain becomes more evident. At present, however, the sense of competition for funds is scarcely evident in Indiana, perhaps as a consequence of the general diffusion of political power in the education field.

Elementary-secondary educational finance is based heavily on local contributions, and in turn on the property tax. In Indiana, as elsewhere, there is talk of taxpayer resistance and of the urgent need for property tax relief. Some steps have been taken in this direction by the legislature through a program to subvent to the communities some of the yield of excise and corporation taxes; however, the primary burden continues to rest on the fiscal capacity of the local real-estate base. This situation bears a good deal of potential for future difficulty in the school finance field. At the elementary-secondary level there is consciousness of the seriousness of the problem but little evidence of the development of relevant plans or a political power base oriented directly to the issue.

The financial picture in higher education in Indiana is also relatively simple. The state has supported its universities fairly well, and this has been the pattern for quite a long time. This is not to say, of course, that there is universal contentment with the level of finance available. Higher education officials here, as elsewhere, are concerned about rising costs. But the atmosphere in Indiana does not appear to be one of panic.

Part of the situation again can probably be explained by the absence of a focus of interest and action in educational politics. State fiscal officials say they deal with the universities separately and see them as separate fiscal entities. They assert that there is little cooperation and little competition between them. This probably means that the budget demands of the universities differ, and each institution's needs are considered individually by the state officials, without a sense of competition among the different universities. The financial process centers on the relationship between the individual institutions and a relatively permissive legislature.

In summary, the basic elements of difficulty are present. Costs in both educational levels are going up, and the fiscal squeeze on the state is likely to get worse. As teachers' salaries rise and enrollments in higher education climb, the demands of both sectors will grow. Now the political system is accustomed to putting them into separate frames of reference, and the institutional arrangements are such that they are likely to remain so for some time to come. Thus while financial considerations may force a closer relationship between levels in the future, either of conflict or of coordination, the matter remains pretty thoroughly submerged now in particularistic outlooks.

Education in 13th and 14th grades

The situation of education in the 13th and 14th grades in Indiana differs quite significantly from that of many other states. Indiana has gone almost exclusively the route of the branch campus; only one public community college exists in the entire state, and it is the product of a set of historical peculiarities. The two major universities have apparently pushed the branch campus idea very vigorously, basing their arguments on both quality and cost. Comments suggest that Indiana University has been the leader in the movement, but that it and Purdue have worked out a mutually satisfactory division of sites between themselves. Indiana now has six branches, Purdue four, and Indiana State one. Most of the branches are expected to offer four years of college-level work.

The branches have grown so fast that they have absorbed the demand for new thirteenth and fourteenth grade educational opportunities, which might otherwise have been a spur to the development of a substantial junior college program. At least for the present, however, the state seems firmly fixed on the branch campus support, with the prospect that some of these will become independent state institutions when they have attained maturity.

The basic question of branch campuses versus junior colleges was debated several years ago by a special "Post-High School Study Commission," appointed by Governor Welsh. The deliberations of the commission were not smooth and the general policy recommendation on branch campuses versus community-controlled colleges was the most controversial issue. The majority of the commission recommended the branch campus idea. Among the most insistent critics of this position on the commission was the executive secretary of ISTA. This is noteworthy because it reveals at least a minor irritant in interlevel relationships.

Vocational-technical education

Indiana's story in the vocational-technical education field is not an uncommon one. Both in program and in organization, the situation is confused, with responsibility divided and not very much going on.

The 1962 Post-High School Education Study Commission commented that a "fresh approach" to vocational-technical education was needed and recommended creation of a new independent state agency to develop it. At that time the field was substantially within the jurisdiction of the General Commission of the State Board and the State Superintendent's Office. The opinion is widely held that those agencies had not been vigorous enough in developing programs.

In response to this recommendation, the legislature in 1965 established the Indiana Vocational-Technical College, an independent agency whose board is appointed by the governor. Its responsibility is to develop and direct state-supported post-high school programs of a vocational character; it functions as both a staff and an operating agency. This new structure is questioned by some, including the state superintendent, who is said to feel that the vocational-technical field should be returned to his office.

The role of the "I-V Tech" is supplemented by that of a state Vocational-Technical Education Board. The principal responsibility of the latter is to oversee the distribution of federal grant-in-aid funds among the various institutions participating in relevant programs. These include local school districts, the universities, and "I-V Tech." Although its function is in good part ministerial, this group, too, is involved in the vocational-technical picture.

The role and relationship of the institutions of higher education in the vocational-technical field is not entirely clear. In some interviews the common fear of university domination showed up in comments about the subject; in others, some said that the universities had tried to stay out of the field except where they offered specific programs. It seems doubtful that the universities will take initiative to penetrate much farther into the field unless to protect particular established interests. ISTA has apparently not taken a very active part in the recent struggles over vocational-technical education, although it has generally leaned toward the development of programs in the local school districts. Labor and agricultural groups appear to have been the main source of pressure on the subject.

In summary, the control of vocational and technical education is not really an active issue between elementary-secondary and higher education in Indiana. It is, however, a latent and somewhat abrasive problem. As in so many other places, vocational-technical training lies in a penumbra, and as a consequence it is at least an occasional cause of conflict.

Teacher accreditation

This subject is a rather weak spot in the information we have available on Indiana, though there has been a considerable amount of action on accreditation over the past few years. Cooperation between levels on revision of certification requirements seems to have been quite effective.

The matter of accreditation and certification is under the direction of one of the commissions of the State Board. A majority of members of the commission must be professional educators, traditionally people active in elementary-secondary education and people from the teacher-training institutions.

Certification has long been a subject of discussion in Indiana. In 1962, a comprehensive revision of requirements was put into effect, and our impression is that these are quite heavy and rigid. The new requirements adopted by the commission were worked out through a series of conferences and consultations that involved a large number of practitioners and professors from public and private colleges. ISTA was an effective and vigorous participant in this development, as was the State Department of Education. Thus the change was brought about through the collaboration of a range of groups, agencies, and people with interests in the accreditation system. Since these major changes in 1962, there apparently has been little effort at any broad-scale alteration in accreditation. Relationships appear to go quite smoothly, but the fragmentation of responsibility leaves the way open for minor irritations to grow, and for the want of leadership, to be felt.

Concluding Observations

Little needs to be said to summarize the educational situation in Indiana as it has been described above. The key phrases have been used repeatedly: fragmentation, lack of leadership, division of responsibility, etc. The sense that things are not happening in the state doubtless grows out of the wide diffusion of functions in the educational field. The state's political system itself seems to lack dynamism, a condition further reflected in education.

In many respects Indiana is now where many of the states studied appear to be; perhaps it looks different from most because it has not moved much from the typical, traditional sets of arrangements and relationships. Either the pressures in Indiana are not so great, what pressures there are tend to be hidden from sight, or the existing loose arrangements serve satisfactorily to resolve problems. As an overall diagnosis, the first suggestion seems the most plausible.

This does not mean that there are no pressures on Indiana education, or that no problems exist that span educational levels. The system and its parts seem so lacking in focus that problems are not defined and conflicts not mounted. This may be an advantage and it may not; lacking attention, developing problems may, so to speak, come home to roost. The legislature apparently has not developed a vigorous leadership on educational questions, and the governor has not played a very active hand. The State

Department of Education is small and the superintendency weak and traditionally not vigorous. The Board is fragmented, its structure such as to spread and not focus responsibility. The Teachers Association finds itself without some of the power it formerly enjoyed, no longer the clear source of initiative on educational questions. The higher education structure is also diffuse, with no central point where demands are brought together to be projected into the larger system. Furthermore, the universities individually and collectively have been strong enough to get a good deal of what they have wanted. Two themes tend to pervade the political atmosphere. One is the tremendous influence, especially in the past, of the Teachers Association. The second is the great power of the universities.

Perhaps the Indiana system is best described as thoroughly pluralistic. The question for the future is whether the state can continue to afford the luxury of so little coordination. Predictions about the future are foolhardy, but it seems likely that Indiana will try to afford it. Few signs seem to say otherwise.

VI. MASSACHUSETTS

The Commonwealth of Massachusetts, under the leadership of Horace Mann, pioneered in promoting public education. However, over the past three-quarters of a century or so, the Commonwealth's efforts to maintain excellence in public education deteriorated to such a degree that a special commission to study and suggest reforms in the Commonwealth's basic educational structure was appointed in 1962. The commission's staff was directed by Benjamin C. Willis, former Superintendent of the Chicago Public Schools, and was chaired by State Senator Kevin B. Harrington. The commission proposed a series of recommendations in 1965 which were recently adopted and are significantly transforming education in the state.

The Willis-Harrington report recommended the creation of three separate state boards to determine and coordinate educational policy. These consisted of (1) a Board of Higher Education, (2) a Board of Education, and (3) an Advisory Council on Education. This state educational structure is still too new to be assessed with great confidence. New relationships and responsibilities still remain to be worked out between the various boards. Massachusetts education obviously is in a state of dramatic transition and transformation, and the following analysis should be read with this fact kept prominently in mind.

The Organization of Education

The Board of Higher Education, though legally within the Department of Education which controlled state colleges under the old structure, is not under department control. The Board of Higher Education consists of eleven members: one selected from each of the Boards of Trustees of the University of Massachusetts, the state colleges, the regional community colleges, and either the Lowell Technical or the Southeastern Technical Institute. These members serve one year terms. The governor appoints the seven additional members and is required by statute to include a member of the governing board of a private institution of higher education and a member of a labor organization.

The statutory purposes of the Board of Higher Education are:

to support, facilitate, and delineate functions and programs for public institutions or higher education in the Commonwealth segments of such institutions, to allocate to them the responsibility and autonomy to discharge such functions and programs, and to plan and develop efficient and effective coordination among them . . .

to approve plans for the orderly growth of public higher education as a whole and of each of its several segments . . .

to review the annual budget and capital outlay requests of the public institutions of higher education, their segments and public higher education as a whole.

The board is required to create an advisory commission to serve as a coordinative and communicative mechanism, composed of the presidents of the various state institutions of higher education, the director of research of the Advisory Council on Education and a president of a private institution of higher education. The Board of Higher Education is also authorized to appoint a chancellor to serve as its executive officer and secretary.

In addition to a Board of Higher Education, Massachusetts has a Board of Education which consists of eleven lay members appointed by the governor, one of whom must be a member of a labor organization and two of whom must be women. The Chancellor of the Board of Higher Education and the Commissioner of Education serve as *ex officio* members. The commissioner serves as the board's executive officer and secretary and is designated the "chief state school officer for elementary and secondary education." The function of the board is to support, serve, and plan general education in the public schools and to establish minimum state education standards in a number of areas.

An Advisory Council on Education also exists in Massachusetts. It consists of nine lay members appointed by the governor, one of whom must be a member of a labor organization. The purpose of the Advisory Council is to recommend policies designed to improve the performance of all public education systems in the Commonwealth; to analyze, plan, and evaluate the programs and systems used by all agencies for public education; to recommend policies which will promote and facilitate coordination, effectiveness, and efficiency in the operation of all public education systems; and to recommend for coordination by the Board of Education and the Board of Higher Education the findings of its analyses and evaluations and the substance of its plans.

In addition to the three boards proposed in the Willis-Harrington report, the legislature established (1) an eleven member Board of Trustees of State Colleges and (2) a Board of Regional Community Colleges responsible for developing policy for two-year institutions of higher education.

Coordinative or Communicative Devices Between the Levels of Education

Massachusetts seems to have built into its new educational structure an unusual interlocking network of coordinative devices between the levels of education. The Chancellor of the

Board of Higher Education serves *ex officio* on the Board of Education. Of the eleven members of the Board of Higher Education, four are trustees of public institutions chosen by their respective boards of trustees to represent (1) the University of Massachusetts (2) one of the two technological institutes (alternating annually) (3) the state colleges and (4) the regional community colleges. The Board of Higher Education is served by an Advisory Commission to the Board of Higher Education which is composed of the Commissioner of Education, a president representing the four categories of public institutions named above, and a president of a private institution appointed by the governor. The Director of the Advisory Council also serves *ex officio* on this body.

In addition to this institutionalized high-level coordination required by the new legislation, there are additional informal mechanisms utilized to insure communication between the public schools and higher education. An unofficial Coordinating Committee meets quarterly to discuss issues and problems of mutual concern. This committee is composed of the executive officers of the several state educational boards. Thus, the Commissioner of Education, the Chancellor of Higher Education, the Director of the Advisory Council on Education, and, on occasion, other representatives of their three boards meet periodically on a voluntary basis in an effort to coordinate educational policies and practices in the Commonwealth. Direct communication among the professional leaders of education is thus facilitated, hopefully promoting greater understanding of each other's problems, personal rapport, and mutual trust.

The most unique and interesting coordinative device is the Advisory Council on Education. The particular relevance of this fledgling Massachusetts agency to the thrust of our study is apparent. The general purpose of the Advisory Council is "to recommend policies designed to improve the performance of all public education systems in the Commonwealth." The council is given two specific statutory functions:

First, it is directed to analyze and evaluate the programs and operations of all agencies concerned with public education and to make recommendations for their improvement and coordination. It is to report annually to the Governor on the status of education programs, with its recommendations.

Second, it is required to submit to the Governor its recommendations for appointment to the Boards of Education, Higher Education, and Trustees of State Colleges. At least three names are to be offered for each vacancy to be filled. Recommendations must be approved by a two-thirds vote of the Council. The Governor, however, is not bound to make his appointments from names submitted by the Council.

The governor, it is pertinent to note parenthetically, at the time of our visit had appointed to the aforementioned boards only individuals whose names had been submitted by the Advisory Council.

The council, like the other new state boards created by the 1965 legislation, has been slow in getting to work. A Director of Research was not appointed until November, 1966 and a second professional staff member did not join the agency until the summer of 1967. The Advisory Council, with its relatively vague mandate to coordinate all education and to serve as a research agency to study educational problems, has had great difficulties in establishing its identity. As a rather nebulous one-man operation in its first year, the council has had very difficult birth-pangs.

The council's future is heavily dependent upon legislative support for and involvement in its activities. Soon after assuming office, the council's director organized a consulting committee of key legislators to work with his new agency.

Supporters of the Advisory Council are optimistic about its future. They contend that increasing numbers of legislators are amenable to the development of such an agency as educational demands continue to escalate. The lawmakers need the facts about education upon which to predicate decisions as to how millions of dollars are to be spent. In Massachusetts, as well as other states, legislators need the type of comprehensive educational expertise and objective data that an agency without vested interests at any single educational level can give. For these reasons and others the development of the rather unique Advisory Council in Massachusetts (as well as the Georgia Educational Improvement Council, the only analogous agency, to our knowledge, in the country), should be closely scrutinized throughout the nation.

The Advisory Council has no authority to enforce its will but it can compel schools, colleges, and public agencies to supply the data it requests. The Advisory Council had just launched its first three major research studies at the time of our visit to Boston. Detailed studies of vocational education, teacher education and certification, and the economics of education were being undertaken under the auspices of the Advisory Council.

As is the case in so many other states, the control of post-high school vocational education is a volatile issue in Massachusetts. The council's study, it is hoped, will help resolve the existing jurisdictional disputes between public school oriented vocational education specialists in the Department of Education and the community college leadership. The study of vocational education is considered by many to be the council's prime order of business.

The vocational education and teacher education and certification studies, however, were not scheduled to be completed until June, 1968 and the Advisory Council in the interim had to become viable and visible, and to justify its existence, particularly to the legislators who must appropriate the funds to keep it alive. The 1967 legislature was asked to appropriate $400,000 for the council and was expected to provide approximately $300,000.

The future of the Advisory Council is also contingent upon the support it receives from the Boards of Education and Higher Education and their respective staffs. The commissioner and chancellor, for example, are both in a unique position to ask the council to undertake special types of studies that they do not wish their staffs to pursue. The Advisory Council, being uniquely responsible for all education, could be very useful to both state boards in conducting studies in areas in which their responsibilities overlap, areas like vocational education, college placement, and teacher education.

Several sources reported that the former Commissioner of Education was not enthusiastic about the creation, and projected role, of the Advisory Council. It was said that he not only objected to losing control of the state colleges to the new Board of Higher Education, but he was also apprehensive about the new Advisory Council usurping some of the prerogatives of the Department of Education. The latter, after all, had hundreds of professional staff members and a Research Division which should be equipped to handle the types of studies projected for the fledgling Advisory Council. Many questioned, and still question, the very need for the existence of the Advisory Council. Supporters of the council immediately responded that the new agency was quite different from existing bodies. It was "unencumbered with administrative responsibilities and was free to study, dream and plan for the future of public education in Massachusetts."

A basic problem of role definition confronts the Advisory Council in its relationship with the Board of Higher Education as well as the Board of Education. Is it logical to expect either the chancellor of a brand new board, starting to develop staff and needing to make its mark as expeditiously as possible, or a commissioner, anxious to consolidate his influence, to delegate to another agency major studies affecting their operations? For example, could the new chancellor afford to delegate his responsibilities for master planning for higher education to the Advisory Council? These problems are by no means insoluble but the *sine qua non* of the council's chances for success will probably be the establishment of close rapport and symbiotic relationships with the Board of Education and the Board of Higher Education and their chief executive officers, the Commissioner and Chancellor, respectively.

Some Major Issues

Vocational-technical education

Post-high school vocational-technical education is relatively well developed in Massachusetts and has competed seriously with the separate and expanding community colleges for programs, students, and funds. Vocational-technical education activities before the implementation of the recent structural changes were controlled by the Division of Vocational Education which was, in effect, an autonomous, very influential division of the State Education Department. The struggle over control of vocational training between the Division of Vocational Education and the community colleges was bitter, each contending that it was better qualified to meet the requirements of business and industry for vocational skills. The conflict was resolved by the adoption of the Willis-Harrington recommendations which reduced the Division of Vocational Education to a bureau under the supervision of the Associate Commissioner for Curriculum and Instruction. It was agreed to postpone until 1968 any expansion of post-high school programs in vocational-technical schools until the Advisory Council completed its study of vocational education. Since the Willis-Harrington recommendations were adopted, the community colleges have received strong support from the associate commissioner. With greater support from the state, their vocational programs are expected to become more comprehensive and less technically specialized. There is strong need in the Massachusetts educational structure for expanded vocational training opportunities in both the community college and the post-high vocational-technical schools. Both types of institutions could expand rapidly and still not fulfill the state's need for greatly broadened vocational and technical training.

The regional community college movement and its relationship to other levels of education

The two-year community colleges offer to large numbers of youngsters low-cost educational opportunities for higher education which would otherwise not be available. These rapidly expanding institutions, located strategically throughout the state, have fared relatively well financially with the Massachusetts legislature, which has granted community college units fiscal autonomy. This has led to some resentment on the part of the elementary and secondary school interests which are not generously supported by the state. The Education Department does not have fiscal autonomy despite many years of effort by the Board of Education to achieve this goal. Identification with the new Board of Higher Education purportedly enhances the prestige of the community colleges. The community colleges are regarded to be in a strong position *vis-à-vis* the legislature as compared with other, older public institutions of higher education. They are already considered by many to be stronger politically than the long established state colleges.

Prospects for the community colleges are generally regarded to be quite favorable. However, they are not being established quickly enough to meet the demand. Some observers estimate that it will take another ten years or so for the two-year institutions to achieve their full growth and political potential. It is expected that as enrollments continue to increase and the base of political support is broadened, legislative support for the community colleges will increase proportionately.

Some serious problems, however, still confront the community colleges. Their academic and vocational programs need strengthening, many require improved physical facilities, and satisfactory transfer programs have yet to be worked out with the state colleges and the University of Massachusetts.

Because financial support for the community colleges comes entirely from the state, some question whether they can be truly community-oriented. It is asked whether state-supported community colleges can provide programs uniquely suited to fulfill local community needs. Since the state colleges are already distributed throughout the Commonwealth, many maintain that these established institutions can readily fulfill the acknowledged need for higher education within commuting distance of the students. Relationships between the community colleges and the state colleges, therefore, are somewhat tenuous and potentially explosive. The continued development of community colleges allegedly has been overtly opposed by the state colleges which fear their growth as direct competitors for resources, programs, and students.

The public schools purportedly also are uneasy because of the rapid development and growth of the community colleges. The public schools rely heavily on local support and taxation. They fear that the community colleges, with strong and growing bases of local support and involvement, may some day need supplemental financial assistance and will then compete directly with the public schools for the local tax dollar.

Fiscal Problems

Elementary and secondary education budgets are prepared and assembled by the Department of Education and presented to the legislature by the commissioner. Community college budgets are coordinated by the Board of Regional Community Colleges which, after its review, submits a consolidated budget to the Board of Higher Education. This board has the overall responsibility for reviewing, synthesizing, and setting priorities for the annual budgets and capital outlay requests of every public institution of higher education in the state including the community colleges.

Education budgets, like other proposed expenditures, are routed through the governor's office. These are reviewed by the Department of Administration and Finance before submission by the governor to the legislature.

Although the various institutional units under the Board of Higher Education enjoy fiscal autonomy, the Board itself as well as the other state educational boards are still subjected to a line-by-line legislative scrutiny of their budgets. There is still bitter controversy between legislators who want to maintain maximum fiscal control and state administrative units or departments which desire financial autonomy.

Some legislators fear that elected officials have already lost control to the great pressures of the educational lobby. They are fearful of the power of the educators who so often ask for a blank check and are "worse than politicians" in competing fiercely with each other for state support. Elected officials are fearful of opposing educational measures because of the general public's great desire for expanded educational opportunities, particularly at the post-high school level.

The bulk of the legislature's budgetary work is done by the Ways and Means Committees of the House and Senate. Since neither of these committees have the staff or resources to develop and analyze budgets extensively, the basic budgetary decisions of a substantive nature are generated by the executive branch of government. The legislature, however, still retains great influence as a reviewing agency and the executive budget bureau officials make every effort to elicit legislative cooperation and approval of their plans.

Relationships Between the Levels of Education

Relationships between the educational levels in Massachusetts appear to be cooperative. Overt conflict for dollars at the state level between the levels has not occurred. Although the state is currently experiencing a dramatic, and in some ways unpredictable, educational transition, there appears to be no danger in the foreseeable future of overt conflict between the educational levels. The general attitude is that the needs of the entire Massachusetts educational system are too acute to permit conflict. Public school interests are too preoccupied with immediate problems of finance and teacher militancy to express concern over higher education. The fledgling Board of Higher Education and its Chancellor, on the other hand, have as their prime objective the development of a badly needed master plan for higher education in Massachusetts.

The lack of overt competition between the educational levels is attributed to the fact that they are supported by different sources of tax funds. Higher education in Massachusetts is not supported from the state sales or local property taxes, but from the state's general funds. Because of the diffusion of the sources of general funds and their lack of visibility, there is no direct competitive situation posed between the levels of education.

Groups Active in Massachusetts Education

Private groups and the public schools

As in other states, a host of private groups have been active on the legislative scene in support of elementary-secondary education. The most influential and powerful of these groups is the NEA-affiliated Massachusetts Teachers Association (MTA). The MTA, with a large membership providing the financial and staff resources for extensive activity in the legislative arena, like its counterparts in other states, is becoming increasingly militant. This militancy is of relatively recent origin and its long-range effects on the Massachusetts educational scene are difficult to assess. However, it is certain that in Massachusetts, as in other states, the relationships between private organizations concerned with elementary-secondary education will never be the same as the result of escalating teacher militancy.

This dramatic metamorphosis of the MTA into a militant and effective lobbying organization resulted, in 1965, in the passage by the legislature of a bill guaranteeing collective bargaining rights to the teachers. This legislation has revolutionized traditional relationships between teachers and the school committee members and administrators who employ them.

The militancy of the MTA appears to have alienated school committee members and leaders of their state association in particular. Teachers and school committee members do not agree on the negotiations issue. Many board members feel that the teachers have become too bellicose and resent the aggressiveness of the MTA.

School administrators, as well as board members, are becoming estranged from the MTA. Historically, administrators, including superintendents, have been members of the teachers organization. The MTA still desires all administrators except for superintendents to be members. Despite efforts to retain administrators as members, the feeling is prevalent in Massachusetts that the MTA's membership ultimately will consist only of classroom teachers. Administrators, it is contended, will not have any influence nor will their interests be adequately represented in an organization in which they will be a minority. Administrators, who at one time considered themselves and the teachers as members of the same team, will now have to identify with either the school committees or the teachers. Most administrators, particularly superintendents, will stand with the school committees.

Private groups and public higher education in Massachusetts

Private institutions have dominated Massachusetts higher education for many years. The existence of schools like Harvard, MIT, Mt. Holyoke, Smith, Williams, Amherst, Tufts, Wellesley, and Wheaton undeniably has contributed to the lag in the development of public higher education in Massachusetts. It is just in very recent years that the University of Massachusetts and the state colleges have begun to emerge from the shadow of the Commonwealth's many prestigious private institutions of higher education. The University of Massachusetts with its embryonic branch campus in Boston, despite its recent growth, still has a long way to go in providing advanced programs and adequate service to a state with 5½ million people. The state colleges are still in a state of flux in terms of their curriculum and for the most part are multi-purpose institutions in name only. The Commonwealth has recently initiated development of a new medical school. It has yet to meet other acute graduate and undergraduate needs.

The growth of public higher education is looked upon with ambivalence by the private institutions whose predominance was once unchallenged. While recognizing the need for expanded college level opportunities, even the wealthiest private schools are apprehensive about their ability to compete with public institutions in an era of skyrocketing educational costs. Many private institutions are fearful that the great public demand for low cost college education will cut into their supply of students.

Political support for the state university in the legislature has not been as strong in Massachusetts as it has in other states. This may be due to the fact that the university has no law school and relatively few alumni in the legislature. However, alumni influence is considerable and growing, but still not as great as it is in a good many other states.

The Massachusetts educational coalition

The Massachusetts Educational Conference Board was organized in the early 1960's with its major object being "to consult regularly as to the status of public education in Massachusetts, its problems, and proposals for its advancement and to make recommendations" in accordance with its Articles of Agreement. Modeled after the New York State Educational Conference Board the membership is composed of the president

and another representative designated by the president of each
of the following organizations:

> Massachusetts Association of School Committees
> Massachusetts Association of School Superintendents
> Massachusetts Congress of Parents and Teachers
> Massachusetts Elementary School Principals Association
> Massachusetts Junior High School Principals Association
> Massachusetts Secondary School Principals Association
> Massachusetts State College Association
> Massachusetts Teachers Association

All members of the Conference Board must concur before the board "may seek funds for gathering significant facts and other research, and for publication of these data. . . ." Unanimity among its constituent members is also required prior to the board's sponsorship or promotion of any program, including legislation.

The Conference Board has focused upon and conducted studies on the state aid issue and played an active role in support of the recently enacted sales tax. The board also supported the Willis-Harrington report and is concerned with implementing the recommendations.

The Conference Board has not been particularly effective thus far in promoting communication between the public schools and public higher education. Attendance at Conference Board meetings by representatives of the Massachusetts State College Association reportedly has not been regular. The College Association feels that it has little in common with the membership of an organization that overwhelmingly represents the public schools and concerns itself primarily with public school issues.

The unanimity achieved by the Conference Board in the successful fight for the sales tax has been difficult to maintain, for the teacher militancy issue has been divisive in terms of the board's operations. At the same time, the board's political strength and its influence with the legislature are predicated on its constituent units remaining unified.

The unity of the coalition, however, allegedly is in grave

danger. At present the board still provides a vehicle through which the teachers, administrators, school committee members, and lay citizens can reach a consensus on some matters, such as increasing the budget of the Education Department and strengthening the department by recommending higher staff salaries and fiscal autonomy.

As teacher militancy continues to grow, the board finds it harder to obtain consensus. Its future may well depend upon its ability to work cooperatively within the new multi-board structure implemented as the result of the Willis-Harrington report. Although the board's future role is uncertain, its contributions to Massachusetts education are noteworthy. The Conference Board played a major role in preventing divisive action when the Willis-Harrington recommendations were being considered by acting as a constructive stabilizing force.

Some Concluding Observations

The MTA appears to be heading on a collision course with many other educational agencies and organizations. At the time this was written, the teachers group reportedly was planning to ask the legislature for the right to strike. Arrayed in opposition to the MTA, in addition to the school boards association and the state school board, were town and city officials and many other groups. It is possible that the MTA has become too aggressive. The reaction of the general public to MTA tactics reportedly is becoming unfavorable and there is fear that the growing estrangement of the teachers from other groups interested in elementary and secondary education may seriously weaken the political power of the public schools of Massachusetts.

The MTA, on the other hand, is critical of the state's slowness in implementing the Willis-Harrington reforms and holds the Board of Education and the Board of Higher Education responsible. In the opinion of the MTA, neither board has been vigorous enough in supporting educational reform. The MTA criticized the Board of Education in particular for failing to seek support and to work cooperatively with "its natural allies in the field of education" like the MTA.

Overt clashes between the MTA and other education-oriented groups may occur within the immediate future. Potential conflict is feared at a time when every effort is being made to implement fully the Willis-Harrington recommendations and improve all facets of education in Massachusetts. Time is of the essence, according to several sources who contend that the new educational reforms will be abortive unless there is speedy and forceful action on the part of the legislature and the three new state boards.

The success of the new educational structure in Massachusetts may in no small way be influenced by the coordinative efforts of the Advisory Council on Education and the depth of the rapport established during the informal meetings held periodically by the executive officers of the state boards. The relationship between the educational levels is still tenuous and the public school leadership is particularly sensitive about its prestige and loss of control of the state colleges. Thus the relationship between levels is very much in a state of flux, but the prospects for the development of coordination through the recently established institutions, especially the Advisory Council, seem promising. If the Massachusetts structure is successful, it could serve as a model for action by other states.

VII. MICHIGAN

The Formal Organization of Education in Michigan

The adoption of a new state constitution in 1963 brought order to the structure of education in Michigan. Section 3 of Article VIII of the Constitution established a State Board of Education (SBE) to "serve as the general planning and coordinating body for all public education and to advise the legislature as to the financial requirements in connection therewith." The board consists of eight members nominated on a partisan basis and elected at large for terms of eight years. It is apparent that the writers of the constitution envisioned the SBE as a policy-making body at the state level with responsibility to assert leadership and to have general supervision over all aspects of education in Michigan. The creation of the SBE places the Superintendent of Public Instruction (Chairman of the SBE) in the position of having available to him a consultative and deliberative body of citizens who are representatives of the people of the state.

There has been a continuing controversy over lines of authority between the SBE and the governing boards of the state colleges. A recent publication of the State Department of Education de-emphasizes the policy-making and supervision functions of the State Board of Education in favor of the coordinating and planning functions. It appears that the State Board of Education is timid in the use of its constitutional powers with respect to higher education. The board will become powerful only when its constitutional powers are asserted and tested, but this does not appear likely in the immediate future. For this reason the individual governing boards of the state colleges will probably tend to continue ignoring the State Board of Education, thereby rejecting control and causing friction between the levels of education in the state.

There is an aspect of SBE structure—composition of the board —that does relate directly to the relationship of elementary-secondary and higher education. Of the eight SBE members, five are associated with institutions of higher education. Many of those interviewed in this study considered these people to have a built-in bias in favor of higher education. Whether this is true or not is irrelevant. The fact is that the state attorney general ruled in 1964 that employees of elementary and secondary school districts were ineligible to run for the SBE because of the potentiality of conflict of interest. This decision was highly questionable because of the board's concern for all levels of education, including higher education. Several interest-group leaders questioned the validity of allowing those associated with higher education to run while excluding educators in the elementary and secondary districts. This matter is significant because it clearly implies the presence of competition between the levels of education in Michigan.

Another indication of the overt competition between elementary-secondary and higher education was revealed during the selection of a new state superintendent in 1965. After many months of searching and considerable SBE debate, the board finally split 4–4 over the appointment of Dr. Ira Polley, a former state comptroller, with no experience in K–12 education. Several weeks later with political pressures building, the chairman of the board switched his vote. The final vote was 6–2 in favor of Polley.

An examination of the details of this controversy over the selection of Dr. Polley show the concern on the part of K–12 educators to insure that they are well represented by the holder of the top administrative post in Michigan education. The Michigan Education Association (MEA) was the most vocal of the interest groups in its opposition to the hiring of Dr. Polley.

The Polley controversy involved one-party political pressure. The SBE was composed entirely of Democrats at the time of the hiring of the superintendent. Polley was extremely influential with the Democratic legislators and for this reason, the MEA and others cried foul play. The main issue in the opposition to Polley, however, was his lack of K–12 administrative experience. In an explanation of their votes against Polley, two board members said that Michigan needed an outstanding educator, with demonstrated qualities of leadership in as many areas of education as possible, certainly including K–12 programs. They felt that there was an ample number of candidates with the necessary qualifications who could, and should, have been considered. Thus there is evidence that K–12 interests are not adequately represented and this causes some friction between educational levels.

There also appears to be a good deal of misgiving about the SBE among the legislators, stemming chiefly from the fact that the board is dominated by instructors from competing universities and seems unable, or unwilling, to coordinate higher education. The end result of the attitude of the legislators is that they tend to ignore the SBE recommendations. One legislator explained that the SBE is ignored by his colleagues because the board cannot identify and establish priorities. Since the board cannot identify priorities it tends to endorse every request even when it is obvious that funds do not exist. This tendency to support all requests is difficult to resist by the board members because they are elected at large on a partisan ticket.

According to several of those interviewed, the only salvation for the SBE comes from Governor George Romney, who takes its constitutional mandate seriously and has publicly committed himself to recommending to the legislature only proposals approved by the board. If a second governor makes Romney's practice a tradition, the SBE will be in a position to control education effectively. If, however, the present trend does not continue, the SBE will be left to preparing factual reports as an expensive information-gathering agency and to making unheeded recommendations.

Fiscal Reform in Michigan

The big issue in Michigan and the one upon which all positive change in education depends is fiscal reform. In 1967 a flat-rate income tax act became law. This is the first new source of revenue in almost two decades. It marks a tremendous step forward, but it is a flat-rate tax and as such has a limited yield. The need for a state income tax was recognized as far back as 1962 by most of the education interest groups in Michigan. The Michigan Education Association's Representative Assembly urged adoption of a state income tax as a source of more adequate revenue. The MEA has regularly supported fiscal reform since 1962, but it was not until July 1, 1967 that Michigan got fiscal reform.

The schools in Michigan are in a sorry financial plight. As an indication of this plight one need only look at the 1967 school aid program. The legislature passed what the public was told was a five percent overall increase in state aid to K–12 schools. Ceilings were then placed on the maximum amounts available for specific funds—remedial reading, school buses, etc., which meant that most districts actually ended up with 2.5% increases or less and some districts wound up with no increase at all. The legislature has come under severe criticism for this apparent attempt to appear generous to schools while actually not helping significantly.

Partially to prevent a one-year standstill from becoming a downward trend, and partially because other branches of the government were also desperate for money to keep operating, the income tax was enacted. The next step will be to make the flat rate a graduated tax, but that may be a long time in coming. In order to get a graduated tax, a constitutional amendment is necessary, and legislators do not believe that the electorate will be willing to amend a five-year-old constitution. Coupled with that fear is the belief that business interests, in order to prevent the legislature from imposing a similar tax on corporations, will block any attempt to provide a graduated income tax. Anyway, most of the monies going to support K–12 and community colleges are local. Those amounts are limited to a share of the total real estate tax imposed within each county for all its services. Even on the local level, the schools face the same problem of competing with other agencies of government for funds to be granted by the state, and in each case all agencies need the money and there simply is not enough to go around.

In 1962–63, with 1,794,045 students, Michigan spent $691,489,615 on K–12 education. The state contributed 36.7% and .43% came from the federal government. In 1965–66 with 1,968,403 students in the same system $918,942,525 was raised; 46.9% from state funds and 1.87% from the federal government. An increase of approximately 32% in revenue raised per pupil expenditure from $385 to $466. At the same time the state increased its contributions to education by one third. That is about all that can be done with available resources, and people are not expecting much more money to be made available from a 2.6% income tax. Local school districts cannot be expected to increase their share of the expenses when millage referenda are being rejected all across the state.

Despite severe shortages of money for K–12 and community colleges, the university system seems relatively immune to financial problems. The University of Michigan and especially Michigan State University always seem able to raise funds for rapid capital expansion and to pay salaries higher than the salaries paid by their rivals in Illinois, Indiana, and Ohio. If the universities had been deprived of money, one might expect that they would throw their prestige and power, of which they both have a tremendous amount, behind fiscal reform. But since they are not affected, they prefer to remain neutral in the approaching conflict. The fiscal situation in Michigan is complex, confusing, frustrating, and fluid.

The Political Structure

There is a formal legal structure to Michigan politics which determines to a limited extent the outcome of the political process. The basic component of this structure is the Constitution of 1963. It is a conservative constitution, not much different from the conservative document of 1908 which it replaced, not modern according to today's standards, and on the whole weak. The parts which affect education are already badly outdated, having done nothing to change the antiquated millage restrictions on local taxes. An article also, incidentally, forbade teachers to strike, which in the flow of recent events has provided an illustration of the sometime futility of formal legislation.

Another factor affecting the formal political structure, in addition to the constitutional framework, is the partisan distribution of legislative and SBE seats. There are thirty-eight senators and one hundred and ten representatives. At the time this was written, the Senate was controlled by the Republicans by two votes (20–18) and the House by Republicans fifty-seven to fifty-three. The Governor was the liberal Republican George Romney.

As was mentioned earlier, the SBE consists of eight members. The first board was solidly Democratic; the present one is split six to two in favor of the Democrats. It was pointed out by several of those interviewed that the SBE was created by a Republican-controlled Constitutional Convention in an attempt to insure at least some party influence in education. With an elected superintendent there was the recurring possibility that the Department of Public Instruction would pass totally out of Republican control. There was considerable chagrin when the first returns showed a complete Democratic sweep on the SBE.

Several legislators indicated that the distribution of legislative seats on a party basis and the fact that one party has a majority may be irrelevant to the Michigan political structure. These legislators likened Michigan to the United States Congress in which the real political divisions cut across party lines. The real split in Michigan is between conservatives (including Republicans who run on the Democratic ticket in order to win election) and liberals (a minority of Democrats and a handful of Republicans). This is an ideological split based more or less on the essential differences between rural-industrial and urban-labor thinking. It is best exhibited by the "Three Jolly Fishermen," a name affectionately given to two influential Democrats and one influential Republican, who are members (but none is chairman) of the Taxation Appropriations and Education Committees of the Senate. These powerful legislators are said by some to determine fiscal policy for the state during fishing trips in the north woods, with outcomes invariably gratifying to the conservative element.

The only serious split in the traditional party-line ideological arrangement is over the issue of fiscal reform. The Republicans are committed to placing the burden of new taxes on the individual taxpayer, while Democrats, at least in public, object to putting the burden on the individual for ninety percent of Michigan's bills and demand that corporations share more of the cost of state government.

In addition to the usual state level political structure, Michigan has a unique organization which should affect the politics of education in the state, but, in fact, does not do so. This organization is called the Michigan Education Council and is composed of all of the education interest groups in the state. It looks on the surface like an association of lobbyists, but by no means does it function as one. The council is merely a view-sharing institution which makes no pretense of reaching a consensus or of taking a united stand. Consequently, the legislature will not take its recommendations seriously. Instead the legislators rely upon informal means of determining the amount of financial assistance needed for educational purposes and the degree to which the state can meet these needs. In effect, the legislature is operating alone when it makes policy in education.

Like the Education Council, the SBE, as mentioned earlier, is not taken seriously by the legislature. A participant in a party nominating caucus and a member of the Senate have said that a seat on the SBE is something of a consolation prize. It is not surprising then that the legislature looks upon the SBE with disdain and smug superiority. Once more the legislature is cast in the position of holding almost complete power to make educational policy.

Areas of Political Activity in Michigan Education

Education enters the political process in five places in Michigan. They are (1) appropriation of money for university operations and expansion, (2) determination of the role and appropriation of funds for community colleges, (3) appropriation of funds for K–12 education, (4) working out satisfactory relationships among universities, community colleges and K–12 districts, and (5) defining the powers, functions, and status of the State Board of Education.

It is the conflict created by the first three points listed above that has caused much of the apparent competition between elementary-secondary and higher education in Michigan. It is strange, for example, that the legislature can find only enough money to increase appropriations for K–12 education by five percent and to provide only a twenty-five dollar per capita subsidy for vocational and technical education over and above the per capita grants to community colleges, but can appropriate all of the money requested for university expansion as it did during its last session. Although no overall planning is done for the universities by the SBE, the legislature can, with the assistance of the governor's Budget Bureau, plan for 1970–75 capital expansion with reasonable certainty that, as in the past, the necessary funds will be found. The explanation for this phenomenon is that the lobbying leadership of the universities is in extremely capable hands. No one talks about the existence of any overt competition between higher education and other levels, but, given a limited amount of money and the fact that one group gets all it wants while the others go lacking, competition, animosity, and frustration must exist. There is no concrete evidence of how the universities outdo their rivals in the scramble for funds.

The relationship of community colleges to other levels of education is becoming a hotbed for controversy. Some interviewees were emphatic in pointing out that the community colleges must decide quickly whether or not vocational and technical education is going to play a meaningful role in their future operations. If it does not, then the community colleges will be brought into a more competitive relationship with the universities, with which, to date, they have been friendly. The reason lies in the fact that academically oriented community colleges would then be teaching students who would otherwise be in the profitable junior divisions of the universities. It is in the interest of the universities that the community colleges emphasize their vocational and technical programs, but the universities have not come out publicly in favor of vocational and technical education, and there are no obvious lines of communication between universities and the community colleges. In fact, lack of communication among the various levels of education is a major fact of educational politics, and probably another reason for the present position of the legislature in relation to education.

The community colleges are caught in a financial squeeze between the universities, which are almost totally state-supported, and the K–12 system, which is only half state-supported and desperate for more money. Most community colleges are financed on a county-wide or multi-county basis. There they compete for millage with K–12 districts. The community colleges are asking for state subsidies for buildings and the expensive equipment used in vocational and technical programs. The K–12 people oppose these subsidy requests because they want the same money themselves. But the conflict is quiet and hidden, and no one is sure of the outcome.

The community colleges also rouse the ire of the K–12 people by stealing their faculty. In an attempt to keep good teachers, boards of education try to support the salary demands of the

MEA and Michigan Federation of Teachers (MFT), but they simply do not have the money at the present time.

The Future of Education in Michigan

The results of this study indicate that the SBE is ineffective. The evidence is that the legislature looks with scorn on the SBE because of its lack of stature and finesse. The universities seem to ignore it and the K–12 people distrust the majority of the members because of their connection with higher education coupled with their lack of knowledge of K–12 problems. But none of the SBE's adversaries can organize sufficiently to take over its management nor have they been able to form a lobbying bloc which could nullify it. Thus education in Michigan is without structure and appears to be almost without direction. This conclusion was supported by the lobbyists, bureaucrats, and legislators who were interviewed for this study. Most interviewees suggested that education was not under any rational control and in fact, that educational politics in Michigan might be referred to politely as extremely pluralistic.

Michigan does, however, have the beginning of a structure for coordinating all levels of education even though it appears that the SBE lacks the stature to be truly effective. It appears that only Governor Romney and his successors can make the board effective. They must give it their support if the legislature is to be deprived of its *de facto* prerogatives in education. As the stature of the board rises, there will be competition among MEA, MFT, and school board members and administrators to control the board, or at least to work with it in some sort of unison.

The big question for the future is the fate of higher education. During the 1967–68 academic year enrollment quotas were placed on out of state students who were charged a much higher tuition. No one is sure whether this means that the universities were given a new source of revenue or whether this tuition hike was granted in lieu of other forms of increased financial aid. While many have said to watch for a conflict between community colleges and universities to erupt over the issue of who educates freshmen and sophomores, one state university president strongly favors letting the community colleges take over these years on the grounds that his juniors with a community college background are better students and more mature people than his juniors who entered as freshmen. If he is right, and if his ideas become popular with legislators, there will be a fundamental change in the populations of the state universities.

It is a certainty that the problems of K–12 can no longer be ignored. The stark failures of urban schools and the clamor for adequate preparation for various forms of post-secondary education demand that these problems be solved. The money must be found now to pay for higher salaries, new buildings, equipment, and new programs.

An inescapable fact is that Michigan is in dire need of fiscal reform. A state, trying to be dynamic and progressive and achieving the objectives expected of it in the last third of the twentieth century needs better and more reliable resources than those sanctioned in the new but only slightly modified constitution adopted in 1963. All the ideological blustering, posing, and posturing cannot substitute for fiscal reform. The state must find new sources of revenue. The most obvious is a graduated personal and corporate income tax.

VIII. NEW JERSEY

The Organization of Education

New Jersey, like Massachusetts and other states, is in the process of adjusting to a recently enacted transformation of its basic educational structure. The New Jersey legislature, with the strong endorsement of Governor Richard J. Hughes, in December, 1966 created a new Department of Higher Education which was to be responsible for all public higher education in the state including the two-year county (community) colleges. Formerly, the State Board of Education through its Department of Education and executive officer, the Commissioner of Education, was responsible for the entire spectrum of publicly supported education from elementary through graduate school.

The State Board and the former commissioner vigorously but unsuccessfully defended the existing structure. They were supported by the state's major public school oriented organizations such as the influential state teachers group, the New Jersey Education Association, the New Jersey Federation of District Boards of Education, the New Jersey Congress of Parents and Teachers, and the New Jersey Association of School Administrators, and also by a number of state college spokesmen. The influential county superintendents were also arrayed against the contemplated changes in the state's fundamental educational structure.

Pitted against these politically formidable forces was the Citizens Committee for Higher Education in New Jersey, a voluntary, non-partisan group composed of leaders from all major segments of the New Jersey community. Chaired by Robert F. Goheen, President of Princeton University, the committee's basic goal was "to arouse the public to the urgent problem of the state's inadequacy in the whole range of higher educational services, and to support measures which will ensure a sound, long-term solution." The *sine qua non* of the committee's program was a fundamental restructuring of higher education which would "free" the public colleges from the jurisdiction of the State Board and the "public school oriented" Department of Education.

The creation of a Board and Department of Higher Education was greeted with something less than enthusiasm by the State Board of Education. A spokesman for the latter described the reorganization plan as "one of the strangest in the nation" but vowed that his body "shall do everything we can to make this venture a success." The new law, which went into effect on July 1, 1967, was criticized for providing for a "great multiplicity of boards with varying objectives but without a decision-making board to resolve the inevitable conflicts." The president of the State Board expressed his hope that a chancellor for higher education be named, "the sooner the better," to guarantee an orderly transfer of power.

Early in April, 1967 it was announced that Dr. Carl L. Marburger would be nominated Commissioner of Education by Governor Hughes. Shortly afterwards, Governor Hughes completed his new educational leadership team by nominating Ralph A. Dungan to serve as New Jersey's first Chancellor of Higher Education. Mr. Dungan, who served President Johnson as Ambassador to Chile and had been a special White House assistant to the late President Kennedy, took over his new duties as chancellor late in the summer of 1967.

Thus at the time of this investigation the new educational leadership in New Jersey was just assuming office, the new Department of Higher Education was in its first few weeks of operation, and the state's educational system at all levels was in a position of dramatic transition. The following analysis of the relationships of elementary-secondary and higher education in New Jersey must be viewed by the reader with the state's transitional situation very much in mind.

Mechanisms of Coordination and/or Communication Among State Elementary-Secondary and Higher Education Agencies

The NJEA and other public school organizations had been concerned lest the creation of a separate board of higher education reduce the coordination and/or communication that should exist between levels of education. The NJEA, in fact, as the price of withdrawing its overt opposition to the legislation creating a separate board of higher education insisted that specific coordinative mechanisms be established. As a result, the New Jersey Education Coordinating Council was created.

The council was established as an interdepartmental body "for the purposes of facilitating the coordination of the educational policies and programs of the state in all fields of public education." The council, which became operational only on July 1, 1967, consists of the following six members: the President of the State Board of Education, the Chairman of the State Board of Higher Education, the Commissioner of Education, the Chancellor of the Department of Higher Education and one citizen member each from the State Boards of Education and Higher Education.

The Coordinating Council meets at least quarterly. It has the duty and responsibility to "review and recommend programs and priorities to best meet the total educational needs of the state" and to "review budgets of the Departments of Education and Higher Education, and make fiscal recommendations to the State Board of Education and the State Board of Higher Education."

Other legislation approved in December, 1966 also was designed to further promote cooperation and coordination between the educational levels. This act, also to take effect on July 1, 1967, made the Chairman of the State Board of Higher Education and the Chancellor of the Department of Higher Education nonvoting *ex officio* members of the State Board of Education.

These attempts to achieve close coordination between the levels of education in New Jersey were in their infancy at the time of this study in the summer of 1967. Thus, the effectiveness of these mechanisms of coordination cannot now be assessed meaningfully but reflect statutory efforts to facilitate and promote interlevel communication and coordination.

Some Major Issues

Post-high school education

The Division of Vocational Education within the New Jersey Department of Education is responsible for administering an extensive program of high school and post-high school technical education. Seven county area technical schools offer a range of high level vocational programs. These institutions operate under county boards of vocational education and are under the control of the Department of Education's Division of Vocational Education. As in other states, there are jurisdictional disagreements concerning post-high school vocational-technical education between these institutions and the county or community colleges. As in other eastern states, county colleges are of relatively recent origin in New Jersey but have increased rapidly in recent years. As of September, 1966, the State Board of Education had approved the creation of fourteen of these county colleges, three in 1963, two in 1964, seven in 1965 and two in 1966. Other proposals for creating county colleges are currently under study. Six of the county colleges were operational in the fall of 1967. Another six are expected to open by 1970. By 1975 it is anticipated that 15 to 17 county colleges will be operational.

The county colleges and the new educational structure

The entire structure for controlling county colleges was altered and currently is in transition as the result of the passage of the Higher Education Act of 1966. Formerly, the Office of Two-Year Colleges in the State Department of Education had administrative responsibility for the county colleges. Under the new legislation, the county colleges will be within the jurisdiction of the new Department of Higher Education.

Article IV of the Higher Education Act of 1966 established within the Department of Higher Education a Council of County Colleges consisting of the presidents and chairmen of the boards of trustees of these institutions, with the Chancellor of Higher Education serving as an *ex officio* non-voting member. The council was created to serve in an advisory capacity to the Board of Higher Education.

Several county college spokesmen stated that most of their colleagues in the two-year college movement in New Jersey supported the creation of the new Department of Higher Education and do not fear that their schools will get overlooked. They recognize the need for coordinated, comprehensive master planning for every aspect of higher education and feel that New Jersey needs a sensible overall plan to accommodate the growing demands for higher education in all of its educational institutions: Rutgers, the state colleges, and the county colleges. The necessary coordination could, in the judgment of the county college leaders, best be obtained by having a state agency that focused specifically on the special problems of higher education, not one like the State Board that spent the overwhelming percentage of its time on the complex issues confronting the state's elementary and secondary schools.

The political power of the county colleges is attributable

largely to their structural congruence with the predominant political norm of localism in New Jersey. As locally controlled institutions inextricably linked with the political leadership at the county level, the county colleges are in the mainstream of New Jersey's political power. The boards of trustees of the county colleges represent a powerful and balanced cross-section of local political leadership. As in other areas in New Jersey, the lack of strong state leadership in determining county college policy has created a power vacuum that has been filled by local political and educational leadership.

The county colleges have also received excellent support from the NJEA and other public school oriented organizations. These groups have endorsed the expansion of the two year institutions as a needed step towards providing broader opportunities in higher education for the state's youth. Relationships between the county colleges and public school systems are excellent. The membership of the county superintendents of schools on county college boards of trustees reportedly has accomplished its avowed purpose of providing liaison between the educational levels. Critics of the public school "establishment" in New Jersey have charged that the county superintendents, who are appointed by the Commissioner of Education, are part of the monolithic Education Department–NJEA dominated structure that has traditionally controlled education in the Garden State. County college spokesmen, however, seem to feel that in most cases the county superintendents are relatively unassertive members of the boards of trustees, but that they do perform invaluable liaison service between the public schools and the county colleges.

There are, however, some sources of friction between the county colleges, and the public schools and state colleges. These are related largely to flexible county college salary schedules which permit the two year schools to pay some personnel higher salaries and thus raid high school and college faculties. Some interviewees believed, however, that the public schools and state colleges do not really mind this raiding of faculty members by county college presidents because it gives them an arguing point in asking for raises for their own staffs.

The county colleges are, in the opinion of several educational officials, a growth operation in New Jersey. They have yet to reach their full potential and are only on the threshold of a period of dynamic expansion. It is predicted that under the new structure state educational authorities will no longer be rubber stamps, perfunctorily approving the actions of local county college officials but that the latter will be subjected to closer state scrutiny. Several members of the legislature's budget and finance staff emphasized the fact that more state supervision was inevitable as the number of county colleges grew and state expenditures for them burgeoned.

The county colleges in New Jersey have sometimes been criticized for not adhering to their multi-faceted purposes. They have purportedly neglected the technical and vocational aspects of their curriculum and have focused inordinate attention upon their college transfer programs. These allegations, which seem to be made against two-year colleges in every state, are relevant to the frictions which exist between the county college leaders and Education Department-led vocational educators in New Jersey. Conflict over control of post high school vocational programs is as apparent in New Jersey as it was in other states visited in connection with this study.

Relationships between the county colleges and vocational educators

County college spokesmen expressed respect for the state's vocational education leaders who are regarded as knowledgeable and able in their field. County college leaders articulated their gratitude for the assistance rendered when they established their first vocational-technical programs. As in other states, however, there is a feeling among county college spokesmen that the established vocational education leadership is not willing to yield any of its post high school occupational education responsibilities to the relatively new two-year institutions. County college leaders report that representatives of their institutions were not represented adequately when the Division of Vocational Education, pursuant to the requirements of the federal Vocational Education Act of 1963, developed a state plan. One spokesman for the two-year colleges alleged that requests by the county colleges for representation on the state vocational-technical planning committee were turned down, a charge which was denied by a spokesman for the Division of Vocational Education. Although the state plan that was developed includes the county colleges, their leaders contend that vocational educators within the Department of Education and their colleagues in the field desire to control all federal programs and equipment allocations under the Vocational Education Act.

Vocational educators interviewed rigorously deny the foregoing accusations leveled at them by the "overly ambitious" county college faction in New Jersey. They defend the existence of separate area-vocational-technical schools, believing that vocational programs inevitably get short shrift in institutions such as county colleges which have parallel academic offerings. The academic prestige syndrome is too strong and pervasive to enable a less prestigious occupational curriculum to compete for staff and fiscal resources on equal terms.

The vocational education-county college issue just described was "hanging fire" in New Jersey. Much, of course, would be contingent upon decisions reached by the recently appointed Commissioner of Education and Chancellor of Higher Education. Some observers believe that the conflict over control of the 13th and 14th grades may become particularly acute in those sections of the state where vocational-technical schools are situated in the same geographical service area as county colleges. There are at present only a few counties in which both county colleges and area vocational-technical schools exist. Several sources were hopeful that the "muted conflict" might be resolved shortly. If not, they foresaw chances for more overt competition and conflict as both the county colleges and area schools expand their operations in the immediate future.

County college leaders fear also that the expansion of area vocational-technical schools might threaten their base of local financial support. Currently, the local freeholders must finance one-half the capital and one-quarter of the operating costs of the county colleges. The freeholders under present arrangements are obligated to support only the county colleges. As the area school programs expand, however, there are demands that local taxes be raised to help defray additional costs. Thus, some observers foresee growing competition for financial support between the county colleges and the area schools at the local level.

Budget Preparation and Presentation

Budget recommendations for elementary and secondary education are made to the governor by the Commissioner of Education. The commissioner, who in the past has worked closely with the NJEA on fiscal matters, with the assistance of the Department of Education staff develops recommendations pertaining to the basic state aid formula. Once the governor's budget is accepted by the legislature, the commissioner recommends to the governor what action should be taken *vis-à-vis* the basic state aid formula for the public schools. The governor then makes the final decision on state expenditures for education within the limits of his total budget.

One of the major functions of the new Department of Higher Education is to coordinate all higher education budgets. The Board of Higher Education is charged with the responsibility to:

. . . receive all budget requests from the institutions, coordinate and balance such requests, and submit a combined request for appropriations annually to the Governor. . . .

The Department of Higher Education thus will have a budget staff. At the time of this writing, however, the new chancellor had just taken office and was assembling personnel to man his new department.

Several persons involved in higher education in New Jersey were skeptical about how effective a coordinative body the Department of Higher Education could be. They predicated this skepticism on the fact that the chancellor and the new Board of Higher Education would have very little control over Rutgers, which consented to creation of the new structure only if its autonomy were preserved. The legislation purportedly was rewritten so that the university would have the protection it desired. The Board of Higher Education is charged with the responsibility to:

> ... make to the Governor and the Legislature such recommendations as the board deems necessary with regard to appropriations that may be required for services, lands, buildings, and equipment to be furnished by institutions of higher education *other than the State University of New Jersey* and make contracts in behalf of the State with such institutions in accordance with legislative appropriations. ...

Thus the Board of Higher Education is in reality a coordinative body for all public institutions with the very important exception of Rutgers. Some critics of the new structure question how the new chancellor and his staff can plan comprehensively for public higher education without having budgetary authority over the state university. The new structure, in their judgment, can operate effectively only if the new Board of Higher Education, with limited powers as a coordinating and not a governing agency, establishes effective relationships with Rutgers.

The role of the governor in respect to education budgets

The Governor of New Jersey exercises great influence over budgetary policy. With the advice of the Budget Bureau he takes the initiative on fiscal matters when he proposes his budget to the legislature at the beginning of each session. The legislature then goes through the motions of slashing the governor's fiscal suggestions which usually remain almost completely intact. In 1966, for example, the legislature cut only $6 million dollars from a $1 billion dollar executive budget. The governor thus dominates the budgetary process in New Jersey and the legislature has relatively little effective power over the allocation of funds.

Relationship between the educational levels and the role of the budget bureau with respect to elementary-secondary and higher education budgets

The basic structure of state finance in New Jersey has important implications for budget control. State funds are not earmarked, but emanate from the general treasury. As a result, the governor determines in large measure how revenues will be allocated among various governmental functions. The practice of "pledging revenues" is commonly followed. It is understood that if the electorate approves a bond issue or if a certain tax is passed that the resulting funds will be "pledged" to a particular service that has first claim on the dollars raised. For example, half the revenue raised from the sales tax was understood to be pledged to elementary and secondary education. New Jersey, according to a Budget Bureau official, is one of only a handful of states that has a one-fund operation, the others earmarking monies for particular governmental functions.

The one-fund fiscal operation in New Jersey means that all functions of government as well as all levels of education are competing for dollars from the same governmental fund. The state budget in New Jersey is thus very much a political document reflecting the viewpoints of the administration in power and the varying degrees of influence wielded by the several lobbies and interest groups active in Trenton.

Despite the fact that the different levels of education are competing for dollars from the same source, namely, the general revenue fund, there reportedly has been little overt competition or conflict. This can be explained by several factors. Both the public schools and higher education have been so starved financially by the state, the fiscal needs of both the public schools and higher education are so acute, that leaders at either level do not begrudge state funds being expended for any segment of publicly supported education in New Jersey.

Another basic reason for the lack of blatant competition between the educational levels in New Jersey, is that state support for the public schools is determined by a fixed formula that is applied uniformly to all districts. Individual legislators or state officials usually do not have the opportunity to push for special benefits for school systems in their district. The state aid formula is rather esoteric and not widely understood by either the public or most state officials. As a result, there is relatively little controversy concerning the application of the politically "invisible" state aid formula for public schools.

Conversely, for the institutions of higher education, budgets are considered individually by the Budget Bureau, the governor, and the legislature. The state officials utilize student-faculty ratios as the basis for determining the state's financial support for each of the schools. Although predicating support on a staffing formula is "unofficial" state policy, it does serve as the basis upon which the Budget Bureau develops its recommendations for state aid to public institutions of higher education. Most recently, Rutgers was supported on the basis of a 12.5 to 1 student-faculty ratio. The ratio for the state colleges was 16 to 1. The lower the ratio, of course, the more generous is state support. Representatives of higher education are thus constantly striving to have their ratios reduced.

Legislative review and appropriations processes

The influence of the legislature is limited because of its part-time nature and the political traditions of New Jersey. The legislature customarily convenes only one day a week from January through June. Legislators receive annual salaries of $7,500. As part-time participants in the increasingly complex task of governing a populous and industrialized state, they are not adequately informed.

The legislature's authority is diluted further by the inordinate political influence wielded by county leaders in New Jersey. The leaders in some counties hand-pick legislative candidates and permit them to serve only one term in Trenton, purportedly fearing that their protégés may accumulate too much power if they are able to build up seniority at the capitol. Legislative leaders are unable to build up political power through seniority. The leadership in the legislature turns over each year, and this also tends to diminish the assertiveness of the legislative body. The Speaker of the Assembly and the President of the Senate (who receive $10,000 annually) thus do not have tenure in their pivotal positions. They do not have the patronage powers which make their counterparts, who usually enjoy long terms in positions of leadership, such significant political forces in other states.

The role of New Jersey's legislature also has been weak because of the manner in which the legislative districts have been apportioned. New Jersey, one of the nation's most urban states, has also been one of its most malapportioned, with rural interests predominating. For many years, for example, state senators representing only 20% or less of New Jersey's population controlled the Senate. A constitutional convention in 1966 reapportioned and enlarged the legislature but in July, 1967 the New Jersey Supreme Court overturned key provisions and ordered a commission to come up with another reapportionment plan for the 1969 elections.

The lag in the legislature's response to New Jersey's education, transportation, water pollution, and other problems is in no small way attributable to rural domination of the Senate. Senators from more rural areas, supporting low taxes and low state services, for many years have thwarted efforts to deal with the myriad problems confronting the heavily urbanized Garden State. There are signs, however, that this conservative stranglehold is being broken. Reapportionment, when it is finally completed, will in all likelihood increase the responsiveness of the legislature to the problems of the state's metropolitan areas.

Although both the Assembly and the Senate have appropriations and education committees, the body within the legislature responsible for detailed review of education budgets is the Joint Legislative Appropriations Committee. This committee makes the key decisions relating to legislative changes in the executive budget. When there is disagreement with the governor, the committee may call in the Commissioner of Education or a college president for a hearing. It must be reiterated at this juncture, however, that the legislature's budgetary changes usually are relatively insignificant. The New Jersey budget is primarily controlled by the executive.

Divisiveness Within the Public School Coalition

New Jersey, like many other states, has had a fairly effective coalition of organizations which have banded together to support the public schools. Called the Princeton Group because it usually meets in that town, the New Jersey coalition is composed of the NJEA, the school boards association, the PTA, the NJASA, and the Education Department. Leaders of the Princeton Group assert that their efforts to unify the legislative approaches of the constituent organizations have enhanced the political influence of New Jersey's public school interests. Differences between the groups in the past have been reconciled privately, and legislators and other state officials have been approached by public school organizations that are buttressed politically by their unity.

Stephen Bailey and his associates in *Schoolmen and Politics* * described the Princeton Group as:

> . . . more of a clearing house than a decision-making body. Here the schoolmen determine where they will agree and where they will disagree. Here also are discussed tactics, general strategy, planning, and execution of various campaigns for school improvements, and here intelligence on the political climate and on possibilities for forward motion is pooled. . . .

There was grave concern expressed at the time of our interviews that the Princeton Group may now be fragmented and that the public schools as a consequence will suffer. One reason for this fear is the growing estrangement of the NJEA from its traditional allies. Teachers in New Jersey, as in other industrialized states throughout the nation, are becoming more militant, and the aggressiveness and bellicosity of their state organization, the NJEA, supposedly is alienating administrators, school board members, and PTA groups from the teachers.

Teacher militancy in New Jersey appears to have precipitated a particularly wide cleavage between the NJEA and the school boards association. The split between the organizations reportedly reflects personality clashes among the leaders as well as disagreements on substantive issues. The NJEA's recent aggressiveness is resented by school board members. They feel that teachers are attempting to gain full control over education from school boards which cannot abrogate their legal responsibilities. The NJEA and its local affiliates, school board spokesmen con-

* Syracuse, N.Y.: Syracuse University Press, 1962, p. 38.

tend, are applying sanctions indiscriminately and unfairly. The NJEA is accused of utilizing inappropriate techniques in school controversies and of "outunionizing" its union rival.

A paramount concern to many of the educators interviewed late in July, 1967 was that this conflict was debilitating the important work of the Princeton Group. In fact, the Princeton Group, which usually met every two months, had not at the time of this writing been convened for more than half a year. Educators fear that public education will suffer as the result of the recent fragmentation of the educational coalition. At a time when the public schools critically need additional state support and are confronted with growing competition for resources from higher education as well as from other public service areas, their political position is being weakened by internecine warfare. They fear that even unity on state aid, the single most crucial issue, will be subordinated to the conflict over less significant matters. The cleavages between the other educational organizations and the NJEA, the most powerful group in the public school coalition, would weaken the pressure on the legislature for more state aid. The tax conscious legislators would enjoy some respite from the perennial pressure of the NJEA for more adequate public school support.

Private Groups and Public Higher Education

The influential role played by the Citizens Committee for Higher Education in the passage of the legislation creating the new Board of Higher Education has already been discussed, as has the significant part played by President Goheen of Princeton University.

Several public school and state college spokesmen referred to what they called the "Ivy League Syndrome" in New Jersey. The state colleges have been neglected for so long that public sentiment favors private higher education. The assumption is made by large segments of the state's most influential citizens that public higher education *ipso facto* is inferior to private schooling. These widely held attitudes about higher education in New Jersey help to account for the great influence exercised over state educational policy by President Goheen and the Citizens Committee. He and other private college-oriented prestigious persons have access to the state's political leaders who likewise are often either products or advocates of private higher education.

Private colleges in New Jersey were accused in the past of deliberately denigrating the public institutions in order to maintain their position of superiority. They and their supporters discouraged the state from making large expenditures to strengthen and expand the public colleges. The spiraling costs of higher education apparently have changed the position of the private sector on the issue of state aid. Even the most prestigious of private schools is concerned about its fiscal position. Most private schools, it is felt, will need generous public subsidies to survive. This new perspective has focused on the need of the private colleges and universities to receive state funds. Cognizant of this need, private institutions, according to several interviewees, have terminated their aloofness and have become vitally concerned with the governance of higher education in New Jersey. Private college interests purportedly supported the creation of a separate Board of Higher Education because they felt that they would be assured of more substantial state support if the educational structure was altered. The State Board of Education, with its traditional public school and state college orientation, it was felt, would not be as likely to acquiesce to private school financial requests as a separate board of higher education. The private institutions would also be much more comfortable operating under a separate board for higher education which would be more cognizant of their problems.

Some Impressions and Projections

Not surprisingly, public school and higher education spokesmen each contend that the other level has the advantage in the competition for state funds. Public school spokesmen maintain that the new two-board structure will make overt conflict between educational levels difficult to avoid. Each board will have the understandable tendency to think of its own needs and overall planning, it is feared, will be subordinated. Elementary and secondary school leaders are apprehensive about the future, for they fear that legislators will identify more closely with higher education.

Legislators and other state policy makers, it is felt, do not have sufficient appreciation of the importance of primary education. People do not identify with elementary schools but are proud of their high school and college bands and teams. Public school interviewees pointed to the fact that while many of New Jersey's regional high schools flourish, elementary schools in the same geographical area are starved financially.

Apprehensions about the state's new dual educational structure and higher education getting the lion's share of revenue are already being borne out, according to several public school leaders. Higher education seems to enjoy a higher priority if the salaries and perquisites of the offices of the new Commissioner of Education and Chancellor of Higher Education are compared. It was pointed out that the chancellor could receive an annual salary that is $2,000 more than the commissioner. The former, unlike the commissioner, also has received an expensive mansion for his residence.

Higher education spokesmen, for their part, believe that the recent riots in Newark will compel the state to allocate disproportionate revenues to meeting the needs of urban areas. Concomitant with cleaning up the cities is the infusion of massive state aid designed to rehabilitate urban school systems. In other words, recent events in New Jersey's ghettoes have dramatized the importance of ameliorating conditions in the elementary and secondary schools of New Jersey's cities.

Despite their own acute and legitimate needs, some leaders of higher education believe that the state's major thrust should and would point towards rehabilitating the cities. Improving public school educational opportunities is a *sine qua non* of these efforts. The close working relationships that have been established between the new Commissioner of Education, Carl Marburger, and the Commissioner of New Jersey's new Department of Community Affairs, Paul Ylvisaker, point to the direction which the state is expected to take during the remainder of Governor Hughes' term in office.

Educators in higher education disagree with the assessments made by public school leaders of their influence under the new structure. They contend that the grass roots political power that can be mustered by public school-oriented groups like the NJEA, the PTA, the school boards association, and the NJASA more than offsets the glamour of higher education. Elementary and secondary schools, they maintain, will not suffer financially as the result of the creation of a separate board for higher education. In fact, they fear that it will be more difficult to gain enthusiastic and badly needed public school support for bond issues for higher education than it was under the unified educational structure.

Interviewees, however, did agree on several critical points. Educators at all levels were unanimous in criticizing New Jersey's archaic tax structure that had starved all state services for so many years. They agreed that the sales tax helped somewhat in taking some of the burden off the property levy. They also concurred in the judgment that the sales tax was merely a palliative and that a state income tax was inevitable. Despite the acute need for funds, however, the income tax will not soon be levied, at least not until the sales tax is partially digested. The sales tax must carry the burden until the income tax becomes politically palatable or at least, not certain political suicide for the government official intrepid enough to make the recommendation.

IX. NEW YORK

The Government of Elementary-Secondary and Higher Education

An understanding of the unique role of the Board of Regents is of central importance to an analysis of educational decision-making at any level in New York State. Unlike the more limited authority of most state boards of education, the responsibilities of the Regents extend to virtually the entire range of education in New York. They govern the massive University of the State of New York and have authority over a diversified educational system that includes some three million public school pupils, 900,000 private and parochial school pupils, and over 600,000 college and university students.

Fifteen Regents are elected by the legislature, with one selected from each of the state's eleven judicial districts and four at large. The executive officer of the Regents is New York's Commissioner of Education who is appointed by the Regents and vested with much greater authority than other chief state school officers. The commissioner heads the State Education Department and not only has responsibility as the Regents' executive officer for elementary and secondary education but serves also as the president of the aforementioned University of the State of New York. The Commissioner of Education's prestige in New York is enhanced also by the fact that he enjoys unique quasi-judicial powers.

New York State's public elementary and secondary school system is an acknowledged leader among the states. The Regents, until recent years, was commonly accused of neglecting its responsibility for higher education and overemphasizing the elementary and secondary schools. Although a network of state teachers colleges and a few other types of public institutions had been in existence for many years throughout the state, it was not until the legislature created the State University of New York (SUNY) in 1948 that public higher education really began to progress. New York, in fact, was one of the last states to create a state university. From its relatively modest beginnings when it had only 29 for the most part undistinguished units, SUNY has grown in less than two decades into a major institution with well over 50 components, including four university centers and two medical centers. SUNY, which includes all of New York's state-supported institutions of higher education with the exception of the four-year colleges of the City University of New York (CUNY), is governed by its own 15-member Board of Trustees which is appointed by the governor for ten-year terms.

The rapid development of SUNY has been looked upon with some ambivalence in New York educational circles. Many private institutions are fearful of the SUNY "steamroller" and apprehensive about their ability to compete with it. Some state officials, while applauding the badly needed growth of publicly supported higher education "to make up for lost time," are reportedly somewhat concerned that their prerogatives for setting overall policy for public higher education may be usurped by the dynamics of SUNY's aggressive expansion. There reputedly has been some talk in New York of divesting the Regents of its authority for setting policy in public higher education and delegating such responsibilities to SUNY's Board of Trustees or some other agency. Influential private institutions of higher education have reportedly supported beefing up the leadership role of the Regents in public higher education to counteract the growing strength of SUNY.

An indication of the Regents' intention to exert its leadership more aggressively in the area of higher education is reflected in a recent organizational change. In March, 1967 the Regents, cognizant of its increasingly complex responsibilities, decided to organize into two sub-committees. One sub-committee will devote its energies to higher and professional education while the other sub-committee will focus on elementary and secondary education. The Regents will meet in sub-committees at one meeting and at the next session meet as a committee of the whole. The members feel that this organizational structure is worth trying on an experimental basis. Whether this format becomes permanent or not, it indicates a serious Regents commitment to involvement in higher education as well as in traditional concerns with the elementary and secondary schools.

Mechanics of coordination among state education agencies

Because it is responsible for setting overall policy for all levels of education, the Regents is by definition a coordinating agency. Although SUNY has its own Board of Trustees and is virtually autonomous in operating its many units, it must submit its long range plans for Regents approval. There appears to be very little consultation at the board level between the Regents and SUNY trustees, but close consultation at the staff level.

The coordination that occurs is focused on the myriad activities of James E. Allen, who since 1955 has served as New York's Commissioner of Education and President of the University of the State of New York. Allen, by virtue of these positions and his responsibilities as head of the Education Department, the executive agency of the Regents, is in a unique position to represent all the varied educational interests in the state. As the chief state school officer he heads the elementary and secondary schools while his role as president of the corporate University of the State of New York makes him responsible for both public and private higher education as well.

Allen meets periodically with the Chancellors of SUNY and CUNY in an effort to achieve consensus and provide advance consultation on the Regents' plans and objectives for higher education in New York State. Prospective differences between the two institutional complexes can be ironed out informally. Allen is also able at these sessions to apprise the chancellors of the needs of public elementary and secondary education. Reportedly, personal relationships between Allen and the two chancellors are excellent and the informal meetings occur in an atmosphere of mutual trust and respect.

Numerous interviewees commented upon Allen's unique and critical role as a middleman not only among SUNY, CUNY, and the Regents but also as a liaison figure for private higher education as well. The private institutions are particularly apprehensive about the rapid growth of SUNY and rely upon the Regents and Allen to preserve the balance between public and private higher education. Several observers commented that despite its recent efforts to tool up in higher education, the Regents has already lost the initiative to SUNY.

Organization of post high school education in New York State

Under the law, SUNY has general supervision over the state's 30-odd locally-sponsored, two-year community colleges. Although the community colleges are under SUNY's supervisory authority, in some respects they are independent and autonomous. Community colleges are financed through a formula which provides one-third state, one-third local, and one-third student tuition support of the operating budgets, and capital costs are shared on a fifty-fifty basis by the state and local community. Each community college has its own nine-member board of trustees, which sets educational policy and operates the institution. A leading community college official believed that this institution in New York "lived in the best of two worlds." Sensing the terrific demands on SUNY, some community college leaders do express concern about obtaining their proportionate share of financial assistance, but there seems to be little thought or talk about separating them from the SUNY structure. Commissioner Allen and the Regents strongly support efforts to improve and expand community colleges, and there was no indication that the Education Department desired either to separate the community colleges from SUNY control or to assume administrative responsibility for them.

This growth of community colleges and the broad mandate they received from the Regents, however, has generated jurisdictional questions over control of vocational-technical education in New York that are analogous to the conflict in many other states over the same issue.

Vocational-technical education

As the community colleges in New York have developed various types of vocational-technical programs, they have intruded somewhat into what was once the exclusive domain of Education Department vocational education specialists. The issue came to a head in New York and other states after the Congress enacted the Vocational Education Act of 1963, which provided support for area vocational-technical schools. In many state departments vocational education specialists with a strong public school orientation naturally thought that the federal funds should be channeled through their agencies to school systems. The Vocational Education Act of 1963, however, did not prescribe specifically at what educational level or to which agencies or institutions the funds had to be allocated. The federal requirement merely was that the expenditures be appropriated to mitigate post-secondary school vocational problems.

In New York, a network of some thirty-five area vocational-technical schools has been established. Although locally controlled, they are under rather centralized supervision by the Education Department. The vocational-technical programs conducted by the community colleges are, of course, supervised by SUNY officials. The problem of coordinating these facilities and programs and avoiding duplication so as to minimize the possible wasting of state funds and resources is of paramount importance to the Regents, which (in its capacity as the State Board of Vocational Education) is responsible for coordinating all the state's vocational-technical programs.

Yet another factor in the jurisdictional picture is the existence of the Boards of Cooperative Educational Services (BOCES). These are, in essence, intermediate districts between local boards and state educational officials. They exist to provide supplemental services to member districts which have the option to participate in BOCES programs or not. Vocational education quite naturally is an important component of BOCES programs and the bulk of the state's area-vocational schools have developed under the aegis of a BOCES.

For many years, efforts were made in the legislature to obtain authority for BOCES to own land, build facilities, and incur debt. In 1967 such legislation was passed with the active support of the Education Department and over the opposition of the community colleges. The latter apparently feared that these new powers might enable greatly strengthened BOCES to cut into post high school education and impinge on the vocational programs offered by them.

Despite this conflict, relationships for the most part between the community colleges and the Education Department have been good, though unresolved problems remain. For example, the Vocational Education Act of 1963 provides that through the 1968 fiscal year one third of the federal funds expended in a state *must* be used for either one of two purposes: operating post-secondary vocational programs, or constructing area vocational-technical schools. Heretofore, these funds had been allocated to the community colleges for their post-secondary vocational programs. Now that BOCES can own land under the new law, some community college people fear that the federal funds they had been receiving might be diverted to the construction of BOCES operated area vocational-technical schools. The Executive Dean for Two-Year Colleges and the Education Department's top vocational education leaders do sit down periodically to discuss problems of coordination with the Education Department's Deputy Commissioner who serves as the state coordinator of vocational education.

In 1966, a series of eight regional vocational education conferences was initiated by the Education Department to establish a dialogue between community college and public school officials in an effort to "preclude harmful jurisdictional disputes and wasteful duplication of the state's resources." Although these meetings did create better understanding on vocational education issues between the community colleges and public schools, much misunderstanding between the levels still occurs. Principles of a general nature agreed upon at the state level are difficult to implement locally in specific situations.

Some interviewees expressed the opinion that the delegation of authority to local community college and public school officials to determine which level would be responsible for various vocational offerings had created program voids. The community college leadership appears to be particularly unhappy about the current ambiguity. There is particular apprehension about the wording of the recently enacted BOCES legislation. It is regarded as "nebulous" by spokesmen for the community colleges who regret that the legislation did not clarify or delineate the respective roles and responsibilities in vocational education of the two-year institutions and BOCES. While the community colleges would like the ambiguities about their vocational education responsibilities *vis-à-vis* BOCES cleared up by more explicit state policy, BOCES spokesmen and most Education Department officials see less of a need for such specificity. They feel that neither BOCES nor the community colleges can or should have exclusive prerogatives over educational programs. Flexibility, not rigidly fixed responsibility, is needed for vocational programs in a large and diverse state in which individual and regional needs vary enormously.

The importance of institutionalizing these relationships and channels of communication and cooperation will grow dramatically in the future as both community college and BOCES operations continue to grow and come to compete for federal and state funds. Local efforts to decide program priorities may well have to be supplemented by more centralized leadership at the state level. Despite some conflict, it is generally acknowledged that the cooperation between community colleges and BOCES has been remarkably effective in New York. Past patterns of cooperation, however, may be inadequate and the importance of coordinated and continuous planning and evaluation may dictate sacrificing some local initiative for the efficiency of more centralized state leadership in the complex and increasingly expensive vocational-technical education field.

The Budget Preparation and Presentation Procedure

Budgets for elementary and secondary education in New York are predicated on a complicated state aid formula. This self-operating formula is based on student enrollments and there is relatively little discretionary authority that can be exercised by budget officials in altering expenditures. Although the basic formula is difficult to change, its ceiling is subject to some political negotiation at annual sessions of the legislature.

Community college budgets, while nominally under the aegis of SUNY are subject to local fiscal initiative and control. The University Dean for Two-Year Colleges at SUNY headquarters in Albany must approve the budget submitted by each community college, and the state then advances its one-third operating share for the next academic year. State dollars for the support of community colleges are derived from the general revenue fund and disbursed to the local institutions. The formula leaves relatively little room for discretionary decisions at the state level on institutional budgets once the initial budgetary development and review process is completed.

The community colleges are in an advantageous position politically because of the way they are funded. Because their state money comes from general revenue funds, the two-year institutions are insulated from a directly competitive position with either the other SUNY units or the public schools. The community colleges have an additional political advantage over other levels of education. Taxes at the local level which support public schools are very visible to the taxpayer, particularly the property owner. In an age of increasing taxpayer restlessness over rising governmental expenditures, the community colleges enjoy the advantage of having the dollars which support their operations remain somewhat invisible. The state share is buried in the general revenue budget, and local support for community colleges also remains relatively obscure, lumped into the county tax bill.

With the exception of the community colleges, each SUNY institution presents its budgets to the SUNY central office where a total University budget is put together and submitted to the state budget director. SUNY, unlike the public schools and community colleges, is not financed on the basis of a written legislative formula. SUNY units are funded on the basis of rather flexible staffing ratios.

The Role of the Governor

The Governor in New York has less power over education and the education budget than any other major policy area. The Regents is appointed by the legislature and its chief executive officer, the State Commissioner of Education, is one of only two state department heads not appointed by the governor.

The executive budget on education is not developed cooperatively with the Regents or the Education Department which formally processes and submits its own budget. On occasion, the Regents and the governor have disagreed on what the state should spend on education. A number of New York governors have taken on the influential and prestigious Regents in fiscal disputes and come out second best. Because of this, as education increasingly has become a more important, visible, and costly state issue, governors clearly have recognized its significance to their political welfare. It is almost essential these days for a state's chief executive to be identified by the public as an "education-minded" official or at least as a "friend of education."

It is reported that Governor Rockefeller for a long period of time has been disenchanted with the Regents. The governor, according to some sources, allegedly believes that until relatively recently the Regents has been a conservative body controlled by an unimaginative bureaucracy.

The foregoing factors help to explain, at least partially, Governor Rockefeller's strong identification with and commitment to SUNY. The governor has the authority to appoint all of SUNY's Board of Trustees as well as four of the nine members of each of the locally sponsored community college boards of trustees. The tremendous growth of SUNY during the Rockefeller administration documents amply his commitment to the development of a first-rate state institution of higher education.

Although substantial increases have also been appropriated in recent years to the elementary and secondary schools of the state, the increments have been relatively much smaller than SUNY's. More than a few public schoolmen share the apprehensions of some leaders of private colleges and universities who worry about the financial implications of SUNY's rapid growth.

The higher education and elementary-secondary budget requests have not been viewed in a competitive context. The public schools and higher education are regarded as separate policy areas with no basis for competition because of the different financing patterns. Elementary and secondary education is financed from the state's local assistance budget while SUNY derives its funds from the state purposes budget. Thus, from a budgetary point of view, education is not treated as a single package in New York. It should be noted that the community college budgets, although they are derived from the local assistance fund, are appropriated to SUNY.

Reapportionment in the years ahead may have a profound impact on the relationships between elementary and secondary schools and public higher education in New York. It is the suburbs in New York, as well as in so many other states, that have had the greatest population growth in the years since World War II. Suburban legislators will be the dominant force in the legislature and this has particular significance for financing education. The pressures for abatement of rising property taxes in the suburbs are growing more acute. Pressure is mounting to tap broader tax bases and to increase the state's share of support for public schools. This would relieve some of the burden on the local property taxpayer. If such efforts are successful, additional state moneys for the public schools might well have to be derived from the state purpose budgets, the source which provides so much support for SUNY. This potential competition between the public schools and SUNY for larger allocations of tax funds from the same sources of state revenue has not crystallized yet. Many believe, however, that such competition is a growing possibility as suburban areas of the state gain additional political influence.

The Role of the Legislature in the Appropriations Process

The Assembly Ways and Means Committee is the legislative body with the prime responsibility for making detailed reviews and recommendations of appropriations for public schools as well as public higher education in New York. Although the governor exercises strong initiative through his executive budget and sets the basic framework of state fiscal policy in his finance message, the New York legislature, unlike its counterparts in many other states, is anything but powerless in the budgetary process. The legislature, and more specifically the Assembly Ways and Means Committee, has had at its disposal in the last few years a competent, relatively large, full-time staff monitoring the state's finances. The executive budget agency does most of the background work in preparing the details of the budget for the governor, but the legislative budget staff has an influential voice in determining fiscal policy.

In addition to the Ways and Means Committee there are several other legislative committees with special responsibilities for education. Both the Assembly and Senate have a Standing

Committee on Education while the Senate also has a Standing Committee on Higher Education. It is pertinent to note, however, that the Senate and Assembly education committees do not really make the high-level legislative decisions relating to education. The most important decisions pertain to expenditures and these matters are handled by the legislative leaders and the finance committees. Spokesmen for the public schools and SUNY emphasized the special significance of the Assembly Ways and Means Committee; one of SUNY's legislative representatives remarked that most of SUNY's legislative program, even matters of a non-fiscal nature, was processed through Ways and Means.

Private Groups and Educational Decision-Making

At the elementary and secondary level the New York State Teachers Association (NYSTA) and the New York State School Boards Association (NYSSBA) are particularly active and influential on state policy regarding the public schools. Both organizations have full-time staffs in Albany, active legislative programs, and are organized effectively at the grass roots level to maximize their political influence. In the words of a member of the legislature, these organizations are "vocal," "articulate," and can exert "enormous pressures" on some issues. NYSTA, the NYSSBA, and other lay and professional educational groups are organized into a coalition called the New York State Educational Conference Board.

The Educational Conference Board has been a most significant entity in New York's educational picture for some 30 years. It operates as a cooperative body of educational organizations and is not widely known among the general public.

The board discusses educational problems on an informal basis and has attempted through the years to find areas of mutual agreement which could be emphasized and publicized through the unifying voice it provides to the educational interests of New York State. The member organizations which constitute the board are the State Teachers Association, State School Boards Association, the State Congress of Parents and Teachers, the State Council of City and Village Superintendents, the State Association of School District Administrators, the New York State Citizens Committee for the Public Schools, the Public Education Association (which is a voluntary organization of interested private citizens devoted to improving the public schools and colleges of New York City), the State Association of Secondary School Administrators, the State Association of Elementary School Principals, and the State School Business Administrators. The Conference Board has traditionally met three or four times annually, often upon the discretionary call of the chairman. It is an informal organization with no permanent staff and virtually no formal procedures to follow.

The importance of the Conference Board as a vehicle through which the public school educational leadership in a unified manner transmits its programs for legislative consideration is very great. The concept of a single board speaking in one voice on major educational issues for many organizations with thousands of members throughout the state has obvious political significance. A proposal emanating from the Conference Board with lay organizations comprising almost half the membership has more impact among legislators than proposals presented by officials of professional organizations whose effectiveness is often limited by the fact that they have vested material interests.

The most important issue confronting legislators and educational leaders is school finance. On this issue in New York, the historical pattern has been for the educational leadership to iron out its differences at Conference Board meetings and approach the legislature united on the basic issue of state aid. This has been an extremely important technique for maximizing support for education in New York during an era when other groups are vying constantly for additional state monies for welfare, highways, mental health, medical aid, and so forth.

Despite the Conference Board's proud history and notable achievements, there is a growing belief in the state that its influence has diminished. Since most of its constituent organizations are upstate dominated, there is a feeling in urban areas and among educational leaders representing the bulk of the state's population that the board is not responsive to the needs of school districts that educate the bulk of the state's population.

While the Conference Board is still regarded as an influential body in Albany, its future effectiveness may well be contingent upon its responsiveness to a new political environment in which it now must operate.

Centrifugal forces are also weakening the educational coalition internally. An organization known as the Conference of Large City Boards of Education, representing Albany, Buffalo, New York City, Rochester, Syracuse, and Yonkers, established in December, 1966, a permanent office and full time staff in Albany. These "Big 6" cities have felt that neither the Education Department nor the existing statewide educational organizations have adequately represented their unique interests or needs. Of perhaps even greater significance is the fragmentation of the educational coalition being caused by the estrangement of NYSTA from its traditional allies on the Conference Board. In New York as elsewhere, more militant teachers organizations, both NEA and union affiliated, are revolutionizing traditional relationships in public education. The growing estrangement of NYSTA from its traditional allies on the Conference Board has the most profound implications for educational decision-making in New York State.

Until relatively recently private higher education all but obscured public higher education in New York, but this has changed with the coming of age of SUNY in recent years. Many spokesmen for private institutions believe that the very future of their schools and colleges is contingent upon the state's providing them with broader forms of financial assistance. Representatives of the private colleges and universities are urging decision-makers in Albany to support their institutions which are well established and have served New York for so many years.

Impressions and Projections

At this juncture there is no conflict or overt competition for tax dollars between the public schools and higher education in New York State. Despite one of the most dramatic expansions of public higher education in the country, there is little or no public school resentment of this much needed growth. The public schools still feel that they are receiving an equitable share of the state's educational resources. Several interviewees remarked that the real test will come when and if the economy slows down and "dollars are tight," and some felt that eventual conflict is inevitable.

There is virtually no contact at the state level between public school interests and SUNY. Regular channels of communication and a broader educational coalition including SUNY "certainly should be established" according to one prominent public school spokesman who feared that elementary and secondary education "would be in trouble in the event of a showdown with SUNY."

The entire future of all these relationships may well hinge upon what final decisions are made concerning state aid to private education. If, as some predict, state restrictions on aid to church-related institutions are loosened, large sums of money may be allocated to private schools and colleges. This will add a new and very significant dimension to the allocation of state dollars for education.

One can reasonably assume that neither the public schools nor SUNY because of their own needs will be favorable toward the diversion of substantial resources to the private educational sector. Indeed, one can logically imagine SUNY and the public schools, instead of competing with one another, uniting in a concerted effort to keep the bulk of new state monies flowing into the public educational sector.

However, virtually everyone interviewed agreed that ultimately a recommendation would be made to extend additional state aid to private higher education. New York's political leadership is not, for the most part, oriented toward public higher education, as is the leadership in states like Michigan or Wisconsin, which have years of tradition behind prestigious state universities. Many of New York's political leaders, unlike their counterparts on the West Coast or in the Midwest or South, are themselves products of private institutions. While supportive of the need to build SUNY into a quality institution, they are sensitive to the needs of private higher education.

Reportedly, the state's most influential leaders are strongly opposed to tampering with New York's basic educational structure. The Regents, with its current powers to set overall educational policy, is regarded as a body uniquely suited to provide the coordinated interlevel educational leadership needed in the years ahead. The current efforts to strengthen the planning role of the Regents in higher education are generally supported. The Education Department's new role is regarded by many as a countervailing force against SUNY. Through the Education Department the Regents will be responsible for coordinating both public and private higher education and will be representing private higher education in overall planning as well as playing a more vigorous leadership role. SUNY would maintain its operational autonomy but would be expected to adhere to the Regents' long range plans for all of higher education in New York. The private institutions, which would be the recipients of increased state assistance, likewise would sacrifice some of their institutional autonomy to the Regents in the area of long range planning.

X. OHIO

In Ohio, education at the elementary-secondary and higher education levels has developed in a generally uncoordinated way. The same is true, in large degree, of their various subsectors. Sporadic change, however, has brought about an unevenness in program development, organizational stature, and political conditions. Thus while there is room for coordination and some models for it, there is also much potential for conflict. The very unevenness of the situation cries for adjustment but mitigates against it politically. Currently, the tension in the system is not overt, but could become so.

The Organization of Education in Ohio

The government of elementary-secondary education

The structure that exists today for the government of elementary-secondary education in Ohio was created by the legislature in 1955 following a constitutional amendment which called for a state board of education. The board has twenty-three members elected for six-year staggered terms from the state's Congressional districts. It chooses its own officers and determines its own rules of procedure, but its powers and duties are prescribed in some detail by law. Perhaps the most important of these is appointment of the State Superintendent of Public Instruction, who serves at the pleasure of the board.

This formal structure has implications for the politics of educational relationships in Ohio. It bears the seeds of its own weaknesses and strengths. Ohio's is the largest of all state boards. It is made responsible by law for supervision of the administration of a substantial array of state requirements and programs, and it is also expected to develop policy within the educational sphere.

The present pattern of operations appears to be much what one expects today in lay board–professional administrator relationships. The board is part time and inexpert; the business is either very routine or technically complex; and the superintendent is "on top of things" by virtue of his competence and full time attention to duties.

The Department of Education in Ohio performs a fairly conventional set of administrative functions, and through the superintendent and board, participates in the development of new state policies and programs. Because the present superintendent has been in office only slightly more than a year, the roles and relationships of the Department of Education appear to be in a state of flux. One gathers the impression, however, that the department has not been a vigorous force for educational change, and it seems not to have had particularly great influence with the legislature or the executive branch of state government.

Educational politics in Ohio are also affected by the activities of a variety of private associations, the most important being the Ohio Education Association (OEA), the School Administrators Association, the School Boards Association, and the state and local affiliates of the American Federation of Teachers. Of these, the OEA is undoubtedly the most important, though it seemingly has not held the power of some of its counterparts in other states. It has represented the central elements of the education profession and exercised the initiative and influence in education that has commonly been accorded them. The OEA was among the groups that promoted establishment of the Board of Education, its goals presumably being to enhance professional control of the policy-making process on the state level, and vitiate the influence of politics on the schools. The OEA and the department have differed over some fairly basic matters of policy. The association is reportedly very powerful with the legislature.

One of the elements in the situation is the development of power in the teachers' union movement. The rising aggressiveness of the teaching profession as a whole, and the militancy of its rival organization seem to have pushed the OEA toward a more contentious attitude. It is stepping up both its political activities and its efforts to establish itself as a bargaining agent for teachers. All in all, no organization—public, semi-public, or private—seems to be in a position to speak for elementary-secondary education in Ohio today. That situation is not inconsequential for the relationship between educational levels.

The government of higher education in Ohio

Higher education has traditionally been strong in Ohio and as in so many states, the public institutions long existed in more or less competitive relationships among themselves. While there was some division of labor among them, the distribution of programs and scarce state funds was a persistent source of friction. In response to various pressures for coordination, a Board of Regents was created in 1963 and given real, consequential responsibilities along with the power to carry them out. The governor to whom the initial appointment of the board fell apparently decided to make it an effective, high-prestige operation with real personal and political strength, and the board in turn appointed a strong, well-known, expert administrator to the office of chancellor of the system.

The board has achieved considerable success, both within and outside the higher education system itself. It has quite well concentrated budget review in its own hands and progressed toward the development of standards of comparison among institutions.

One outside observer of the legislative scene commented that the university presidents "are not much in evidence in Columbus any more." The Regents are also said to be strong with the governor and strong with the legislature. While they do deal with the Director of Finance, their dealings are apparently on a friendly and mutually supportive basis. The board and its staff have established direct legislative relationships, both with individuals and with key committees. Undoubtedly some of the board's success grows out of the fact that it has so effectively taken the heat off the legislators in the higher education field. The extent of its power is difficult to gauge, but it is without doubt great.

Issues in the Relationship of Elementary-Secondary and Higher Education

Financing the schools and colleges

Despite its substantial economic capacity Ohio does not support its public schools particularly handsomely, and it leans heavily on the local property tax for operating revenue. A similar general comment can be made about higher education in Ohio. That is to say, the industrial and social base of the state is such that the demands on higher education are great and its support potential is also high. While expenditures for higher education have increased very substantially in recent years, and while the state has a well-established system, it has not been generous with the universities when compared with similar states.

State support for local school districts for operating expenditures in Ohio comes through a foundation program whose details are fixed by the legislature. In total, the state provides about 30 percent of district operating expenditures. The process of decision on school finance at the state level is essentially a two-step matter, one involving the consideration of the foundation program and the other the provision of funds to carry it out. Each biennial session of the legislature is obliged, not legally but by political circumstances, to give some attention to the overall program.

While we do not have the full picture of the political circumstances surrounding these decisions, a few aspects of it are apparent. The institutional condition of education being what it is, it seems as though the elementary-secondary sector has not been particularly cohesive and has tended to lack forceful common leadership. More specifically, in Ohio it appears that the state education officials have not usually taken an aggressive position on state support, although they have made recommendations to raise the foundation support level. The OEA has also worked in this direction, though its specific recommendations have not recently been coordinated with those of the state office. The school people tend to feel that the executive branch has not been particularly supportive of elementary-secondary education, but that the board and department have been left to go their own way. In the circumstances, the legislature is left relatively free to make decisions on educational finance. It purportedly listens to the OEA, but the diffuseness of political power in the field gives the legislators much latitude within which to move. The legislature is, of course, subject to all kinds of demands for money which it must ultimately accommodate within a single framework of fiscal capacity. Focussed political pressure in such a setting doubtless accounts for a great deal, but the political power of elementary-secondary education has not been well-focussed. Furthermore, the general atmosphere of state government in Ohio has been rather conservative about spending. These factors are probably the ones that tend to account for the rather low level of state support. The establishment of the Board of Regents has brought about a substantial change in the processes of financing higher education. The system is still new, and its impact is yet developing, but it has moved very quickly to change the conditions of decision-making. When the board was established it was given responsibility for reviewing the appropriations requests of the state supported colleges and universities and submitting recommendations to the director of finance and the chairman of the two legislative finance committees. Thus it started with direct links to two key spots in the fiscal process.

The board has apparently used its potential effectively, and its initiative has been well received. It has secured legislation to change the basis on which higher education finance was handled, leaving institutions their income from fees and paying state support in monthly lump sums. This legislation created a kind of autonomy for the individual institutions and at the same time doubtless strengthened the board's hand in the planning, appropriations, and review processes. The legislature's act was symbolic of its trust in the new board system. Higher education appears to have achieved both focussed, aggressive leadership and the favor of the state political structure.

Both elementary-secondary and higher education are under pressure to expand services and raise quality. Both are also dependent on money drawn from the general funds of the state for a minor but critical portion of their operating expenses. Elementary and secondary education is under further pressure from the forces that would reduce the local property tax burden. In the circumstances it would be no great surprise if a sense of competition for funds between elementary-secondary and higher education did exist. Explorations of the question suggest that such feelings are latent but not manifest. There appears to be some fear among public education people of the growing strength of higher education, and some feeling that the public schools are suffering or may suffer as a result. The feeling is not uncommon that elementary-secondary education has not been accorded its deserved share of political support.

These comments are not by any means intended to suggest that interlevel conflict is inevitable. The probabilities of sustained conflict on a clear-cut institutional basis are low. However, the differential development of the two sectors seems likely to redound to the advantage of higher education. In the light of the achievements of the higher education structure, integration across levels is not unthinkable, and if such integration does come about it is likely to be under the leadership of the higher education sector.

Education in the 13th and 14th grades

Before the development of the Board of Regents, education in the 13th and 14th grades was handled through branch campus operations of the established universities, most of them offering two years of general college work. By 1965 these numbered 35, and the policy of the board has been to encourage and extend their use to meet enrollment needs.

The effect of the development of public 13th and 14th grade education through branch campuses has been to keep most of it in the hands of the university system. With the universities moving to fill needs, the junior college concept has made little headway in Ohio. Both the situation with respect to need for institutions and the political-educational atmosphere mitigate against junior or community college growth. In this fashion, Ohio seems to have forestalled much of the potential controversy over the control and character of 13th and 14th grade education.

A related problem, and one that can usefully be discussed in the present context, is the matter of standards of admission to higher education. The question, simply put, is whether secondary school graduates are to be excluded from the public institutions of higher education and if so on what basis. Ohio law now provides that "a graduate of the twelfth grade shall be entitled to admission without examination to any college or university which is supported wholly or in part by the state. . . ." The Regents have promoted the interpretation that the right to admission is a right to admission to the *system*, not to any particular component of it. Thus the groundwork is laid for differential academic use of the various kinds of facilities in the system. A Master Plan developed by the Regents envisions severely limited freshman and sophomore enrollments on central university campuses, these being turned primarily to upper division, graduate and professional programs. A large share of lower division education would then be done through the branch campuses. This plan has economic appeal to both the public and the consumer, for, as we have noted elsewhere, the system will be large and dispersed enough to place a lower division institution within commuting reach of virtually every student in the state. By maintaining open enrollment in branches, the university system can reap political rewards, can sustain the state's democratic tradition on admissions, and can develop central campuses on selective and specialized bases.

Vocational and technical education

In Ohio, as in other states, issues arising out of the vocational and technical education field are vexations to nearly everyone involved. The matter of control of vocational-technical education is one of the main questions at issue in the relationship between elementary-secondary and higher education levels. Several vocational-technical programs are in operation in Ohio. The high schools offer a variety of courses, under the general supervision of a division of the State Department of Education. Also under the responsibility of the department are special joint vocational school districts, three of which have been established under state legislation designed to provide training in skills relevant to the economic patterns of various areas of the state.

In addition, vocational-technical education is to be found in technical institutes, community colleges, and branch and main university campuses. The technical institutes and area technical schools fall in the penumbra between secondary and higher education, as they may offer two-year associate degrees if they meet standards set out by the Board of Regents. The legislature appears to be essentially permissive to the Regents if they wish to move into the vocational-technical field.

It is in this penumbra that the possibilities for conflict arise. The inception of the Board of Regents has given impetus to some moves toward clarification. A "Memorandum of Understanding" negotiated by the board and the Department of Education points directions toward a division of responsibilities. The key is an attempt at distinction between vocational and technical education. According to the understanding, vocational programs are to be the responsibility of the high schools and the Department of Education, technical programs the responsibility of the community colleges, technical institutes, and university branches under the Board of Regents. At best, the definitions offered in the agreement are vague and open-ended. However, the memorandum symbolizes the interaction of the governing bodies and their staffs, and their desires to find common bases for action. While it may not afford a very satisfactory response to the problem in the abstract, in the pragmatic world of piecemeal challenges it might prove to be a substantial aid to conflict management.

Accreditation of teacher training programs

In Ohio the supervision of teacher education programs in both public and private colleges and universities is a responsibility of the State Department of Education, as is the certification of teachers themselves. A special division of the department performs this task, operating under the aegis of the state board. In light of the fact that from 25 to 50% of the undergraduate enrollments of the state-assisted institutions of higher education are in teacher training programs, this is obviously a field in which the interests of the Regents and the department overlap.

The subject of teacher education has been under intensive and sometimes heated discussion in this country during recent years. The heat generated by the subject has not been especially evident in Ohio, though some of the basic problems are present there as in probably every other state. Generally, the fundamental issue seems to be the extent to which "professional education" (*i.e.*, training in pedagogy and related matters) is to dominate the required curriculum for would-be teachers. At least outside the schools of education most higher education people who have interested themselves in the matter have pushed for more general education and subject-matter content in the certification program. Ohio's requirements are moderate as these things go. The state also appears to put few highly specific requirements on the training programs. Nonetheless, to the extent that there are state requirements at all, the state limits the flexibility of college programs and the control of the colleges over them.

This, then is a potential source of friction, but one that can be controlled by the joint endeavors of the parties concerned. The State Department has apparently been conscientious about consulting higher education on certification and accreditation programs, though it does not have ample staff resources. In the nature of things, however, the teacher education program is an area where neither elementary-secondary nor higher education interests are likely to want some major confrontation. The general climate of education is such that change in that area is probable, but unless unforeseen pressures develop, change may be accomplished by processes of adjustment and accommodation.

Some Concluding Observations

This report began on the theme that the dominant fact in the Ohio educational scene is the uneven distribution of political thrust and influence between higher and elementary-secondary education. This is partly accounted for by the extraordinary success of the coordinating structure of the universities, and partly by the degeneration of traditional alliances at the elementary-secondary level. All such matters are relative and temporary, of course. There is vigor among the public school people, and they have far more of the raw ingredients of political power. But public education at the elementary-secondary level is generally beleaguered and rather disorganized today, and Ohio presents no exception.

The consequence for the decision-making system is unevenness of attention and lack of coordination in the elementary-secondary sector. Despite the magnitude of the needs of the public schools, they are not pressed with as much force and focus as one might expect, and probably for this reason tend to be handled in a partial and piecemeal fashion. Meanwhile, the higher education system can identify its needs and present them in a much neater and tidier package.

What is said here is not meant to suggest that the needs of elementary-secondary and higher education are necessarily in conflict, that the two are in direct competition for limited and earmarked resources. Indeed, they are essentially complementary, essentially parts of a common fabric of social problems. The point is that even if they are thus, they are also separated, however artificially, according to the perspectives through which political problems are viewed. This separation is given substance in the fact that the two sectors are under different systems of control. In politics, therefore, their needs are defined, aggregated, and processed differently, up to the top decision-making level. Thus it is possible, natural, and even easy for the legislature and governor to treat the needs of the different sectors separately.

As the fiscal pressure continues or, more probably, as it increases, the potential for open conflict between elementary-secondary and higher education also grows, exacerbated by other frictions between the two levels. There are several courses that interlevel relationships may take: (1) The legislature may equip itself, with executive branch help or leadership, to serve a genuinely coordinative role. (2) Informal coordination between sectors, for which there is already some precedent, may temper potential conflicts. (3) A new structural coordinative mechanism for all education might be introduced into the picture. This approach seems politically unlikely, but it has occurred as a possibility to some concerned people. (4) Higher education, because of its political strength, might dominate the scene where conflicts arise, with elementary-secondary education handled quietly, *ad hoc*, and piecemeal. This list does not exhaust the possibilities, but it includes the courses of events that seem most likely.

XI. PENNSYLVANIA

Public education in Pennsylvania seems to be in mild turmoil. This situation has permeated all levels of education as well as all facets of the state government including the governor's office and the legislature. The apparent unrest concerning education is focussed in several issues which have drawn public attention. These issues include (1) a Master Plan for higher education, (2) a community college versus Pennsylvania State University branch campus conflict, (3) an aid to nonpublic schools bill and (4) a very controversial intermediate unit reorganization plan for the public schools. Before these issues can be explored in detail it is necessary to understand Pennsylvania's unique government for elementary-secondary and higher education.

The Organization of Education

Since 1963, education in the Commonwealth of Pennsylvania has been governed by a single State Board of Education. Prior to that year a State Council of Education had been responsible for educational decision-making. Dissatisfaction with the council grew for several reasons. First, higher education was rather poorly represented on the nine member, gubernatorially appointed council. Attempts were made before 1963 to create a separate state council of higher education but these attempts were opposed by those who felt that education in Pennsylvania should be an integrated, kindergarten through graduate school system and that this could be accomplished only by one policy-making board at the state level. The old State Council also was criticized because of the powerful position it created for the State Superintendent of Public Instruction.

In 1961, Governor David Lawrence, who was aware of a stagnant educational situation, appointed a Committee of One Hundred for Better Education which was charged with making recommendations for the general improvement of education in the state. In making its recommendations, the committee alluded to dissatisfaction with the State Council. It is no secret that there was some jealousy between the levels of education because of the unfair representation afforded elementary-secondary education on the old State Council. With this in mind, the committee recommended the establishment of a State Board of Education composed of two councils. One, known as the Council for Basic Education deals with elementary-secondary education, and the other, known as the Council of Higher Education, deals with programs and policies in the field of higher education. Each is composed of seven members appointed by the governor. When the two councils meet together, they function as a state board and have authority in all decisions involving major educational policy in the state. The state board as a whole reviews and ratifies, or rejects the actions of the separate councils, thereby providing coordination between levels of education.

Before Governor William Scranton presented the committee's recommendation to the legislature in 1963, he added the idea of three members-at-large. The present state board is accordingly composed of the two seven member councils plus three at-large members. The power of the superintendent was diminished by making him a non-voting chief executive officer.

In its brief existence the state board has accomplished several impressive tasks. It has developed a Master Plan for higher education, sponsored studies of the state colleges and vocational-technical education, developed standards for school district reorganization, and begun a study of the quality of education in the state. There appears, however, to be a steadily growing undercurrent of unhappiness with the state board on the part of some legislators and school people. Before this criticism of the state board is examined, some other aspects of the government of education need to be pointed out.

The Department of Public Instruction (DPI), a fairly typical structure, is basically the administrative arm of the State Board of Education. The superintendent is the chief executive officer of the DPI and serves in this same role for the State Board of Education. The rather large bureaucracy is organized into offices of basic and higher education, each headed by a deputy superintendent.

The Pennsylvania higher education system (if indeed, it can be called a system) is very loosely organized structurely. There is no state university *per se*. Pennsylvania State University, along with the University of Pittsburgh and Temple University are referred to as state-related universities. These institutions receive state appropriations and offer low tuition education to residents, and carry responsibilities for various state-mandated programs.

In addition to the state-related universities, Pennsylvania has fourteen state-owned colleges with boards of trustees appointed by the governor. These will be discussed more fully under the section on the Master Plan for Higher Education.

The state also has a system of community colleges which is under the control of the State Board of Education to the degree that the board is empowered to approve or disapprove plans for improvement and set standards for the colleges. Each community college, however, is controlled by a local board. The state provides one third of the operating budget and one half of the capital expenses of these colleges.

Financing Public Education in Pennsylvania

Support for elementary-secondary education in Pennsylvania is based on several principles. The most important factor of concern to the legislature and to all citizens of the state is the retention of the principle of equalization of educational opportunity. To insure the maintenance of this principle the legislature has established a formula for support of the public schools which essentially provides a 50–50 partnership between the state and the local school district. The state subsidizes the local districts at a level up to one half of the average statewide expenditure per pupil. In addition, the state recognizes that densely-populated and sparsely-populated areas have special fiscal problems that warrant additional contributions.

For many years the colleges and universities in the state have been totally uncoordinated in their effort to secure state aid. It has been only recently that some order has been brought to this matter. Now, with the recommendations of the Master Plan, there seems to be agreement that serious attention should be given to coordination of the various segments of higher education.

The governor's budget secretary is an important figure in the appropriations process for the state colleges, with considerable influence over the amount of money that will eventually be appropriated for any particular school. There appears to be mixed feeling toward the power of the budget secretary. Most respondents realize that the budget secretary is making budget decisions for education, but that the overall decisions have to be made and that the source is an appropriate one. Others, on the other hand, feel quite strongly that the budget secretary should not make decisions concerning the budget for educational purposes, particularly in the area of budget cuts for recommended items. It is interesting to note that the budget secretary dislikes being in a position of being accused of controlling education by budget decisions. He claims that the Superintendent of Public

Instruction merely passes budget requests of the separate institutions on to the governor's office and that he, as budget secretary, is forced into this unpleasant decision-making role. The secretary emphasizes that the recommendations made in the Master Plan, if accepted, will bring order to the process by introducing the formula approach to the determination of appropriations. Interlevel competition for funds transcends the entire budget-making procedure because the budget secretary must continually keep in mind the needs of elementary-secondary education as he considers the requests of higher education.

Educational Issues in Pennsylvania

The Master Plan for Higher Education

As soon as it was created, the State Board of Education was directed by the legislature to develop a Master Plan for higher education, an enterprise stimulated by the report of the Committee of One Hundred which asked for an increase in the attention paid to higher education. The legislative act creating the State Board of Education in 1963 directed the board immediately to "develop a Master Plan for Higher Education in the Commonwealth, including a system of community colleges as provided by law." The final report was presented to the board in July, 1966.

The Master Plan recommended a set of steps designed to bring order to the higher education system. Its suggestions included defining the responsibilities of the segments of higher education, presenting a rationale for fiscal support, refining procedures for coordination, and presenting bases for the encouragement of private institutions. The question is, however, whether these recommendations will be translated into legislation.

The Master Plan for Higher Education calls for both legislative and administrative action, but neither type is developing very rapidly. The lack of administrative action is due in part to the rapid turnover in the office of Superintendent in the past two years. With the appointment of Dr. David Kurtzman, former Chancellor of the University of Pittsburgh, as Superintendent, this problem has been surmounted. The reasons underlying the lack of legislative action are considerably more complicated. An explanation of these reasons will not only help to account for the lack of legislative action but will also help to point out state board-legislature relationships and the relationships between elementary-secondary and higher education in Pennsylvania.

There is general agreement among legislators, state board members and professional educators that the lack of legislative action on the Master Plan is directly related to the legislature's lack of confidence in the state board. Therefore, the solution to translating the Master Plan recommendations into legislation lies in the ability of the state board to gain the confidence of the legislature and of the willingness of the legislature to let the board develop those areas in which administrative action, rather than legislation, is required.

The main reason for lack of legislative confidence in the state board seems to stem from the legislators' mistrust of appointed boards in general. This accounts for the fact that there is little communication between the two bodies and for the fact that the legislators feel that the board's power should be minimized. Some legislators do recognize, however, that the state board could eventually act as a shock absorber and in effect, take the pressure off of legislators on certain issues. The Highway Commission seems to perform this function. But education in the state has been much harder to define and more difficult to sell than highways, particularly in rural areas. There is some hope that confidence in the board will come with age and sophistication.

The state board leaders themselves agree that the board is steeped in trivia and often does not get around to anything significant. One recent meeting was devoted entirely to a discussion of a secondary school boundary decision. Some observers contend that the college presidents and county superintendents have tried deliberately to prevent the board from considering major problems. In this way the colleges maintain their autonomy and the county superintendents do not lose political power. It is difficult to find any concrete evidence of such a planned strategy to undermine the state board.

Another reason that to date the Master Plan has not been

translated into legislation is the fact that the Pennsylvania legislature is rather unwilling to allow much action on higher education to get out of its hands. This fact, coupled with the point that this is the fourth master plan in recent years that has come out just as the governor was about to leave office, further explains why the legislature can ignore the state board's plan.

Even though there is considerable dissatisfaction with the speed with which the Master Plan is being enacted, eventually its proposals will be brought to the legislature. As these changes are considered by the legislature, the competition between elementary-secondary and higher education will become more pronounced. It was mentioned earlier that there has always been some competition between educational levels, often manifest in attempts to establish a separate Board of Higher Education. The new Superintendent of Public Instruction strongly advocated the establishment of a separate board of higher education. He also has suggested changing the name of the Department of Public Instruction and the title of Superintendent. The present designations, he claims, date back to the days of unfair emphasis on basic education. The new superintendent is a former college president whereas his predecessors were clearly identified with the elementary-secondary level. He believes that higher education has suffered neglect, a neglect countenanced by former superintendents. In statements prior to his taking office, he emphasized that the major thrust of the Department of Public Instruction in the next few years must be in higher education.

The Master Plan has promoted the idea that providing a fiscal base for education continues to be one of the most important responsibilities of state government. There is concern that although the requirements in the area of basic education have in the past been the prime responsibility, the growing needs of higher education, emphasized in the Master Plan, must now receive more serious consideration. It seems very likely that for this reason, too, there will be increasing competitiveness between the proponents of basic education and higher education as a result of the Master Plan.

The emphasis in the Master Plan on doctoral programs and professional work is certain to split further the levels of education in their competition for funds. Today, public support for education beyond the high school is considered a basic need. The Master Plan dramatized the argument that there should no longer be proponents of both basic education and higher education; instead, all groups should support a cooperative relationship between the levels, with education as a whole identified as their cause. This argument probably is unrealistic at present because of the structure of education in the state, but it is the hope of many for the future. Unfortunately, priorities are still established within levels of education and a competitive atmosphere tends to persist.

Education in the 13th and 14th grades

For some time now a major controversy has been brewing regarding the government of education in the thirteenth and fourteenth grades. In general terms, the problem centers on the relationship between the State Board of Education and Pennsylvania State University. The problem is serious because it transcends levels of education and causes overt conflict. The real question is whether the State Board of Education is more powerful than the independent Pennsylvania State University. The problem has manifested itself in a controversy between Penn State and the state board over whether Pennsylvania can support two separate systems at grades thirteen and fourteen. Specifically the question revolves around an action by the state board to curtail expansion of Penn State branch campuses. The matter came to a head when the state board asked the legislature to cut from Penn State's budget any funds earmarked for a new off-campus center in Delaware County.

In this Delaware County incident, the board adopted a resolution urging that the Penn State budget be cut on the grounds that Penn State's action in establishing the branch campus was a unilateral decision contrary to state board policy. The resolution pointed out that Penn State had gone ahead with plans to open a Delaware County campus even though the board had already endorsed the establishment of a community college in the county. In the past, the board has been all but powerless to stop what it says are blatant defiances of its policies by Penn

State. It appears that this time the board has found an effective technique for keeping Penn State under control. The community college-branch campus conflict has provided the legislators with a good excuse for acting on their disenchantment with expenditures for higher education, particularly since it came at a time when legislators of both parties were advocating budget cuts.

Unquestionably, Pennsylvania's system of higher education needs some coordination and unity, and the state board provides the best hope now for getting some coherence in the system. At the present time the board has adequate powers in basic education. Other than the willingness of the legislature to allow it to develop a community college program, it has only limited power in higher education. The Delaware County case is significant because it is a test of power for the state board in an area where it does not pretend to enjoy much power.

Support for non-public schools

One of the most controversial bills of the 1967 session of the Pennsylvania legislature was House Bill 1136 which would create a state Non-Public School Building Authority with powers to purchase secular educational services from non-public schools within the state. The main provision of this bill, which at this writing has not been acted upon, is to establish authority to spend public funds to pay teachers in non-public schools for the time they spend teaching the secular subjects. The controversy created by this bill is of interest because (1) it illustrates the competition for funds used for education and (2) it shows how the educational interest groups in the state can mobilize forces for a cause.

The non-public schools, and particularly the Catholic schools, in Pennsylvania are in a state of crisis. They are beset by such mounting financial difficulties that some of them may be forced to close or reduce their services. If this should happen there will be a big shift of pupils into the public schools, which are already burdened by financial problems, overcrowding, and teacher shortages in many areas.

At present there are about 600,000 pupils, or twenty-three percent of all children in K–12 education in the state, enrolled in non-public schools. According to one study, this saves the taxpayers more than $350 million a year in operating costs for the public schools.

Because the non-public schools are in dire financial difficulty, it is easy to understand why they are attempting to acquire money from the state to reduce their costs. The mere introduction of House Bill 1136 touched off severe opposition from most of the education interest groups in the state. These groups presented a united front on the issue which is not uncommon in Pennsylvania. (There is a coalition of the Pennsylvania State Education Association, the PTA, and the Pennsylvania School Boards Association that often emerges on an *ad hoc* basis to deal with specific issues.) The gist of their arguments is based on the assumption that there can be dual systems of public and non-public schools but that present fiscal facts regarding education quickly dispel any illusion that public education is so affluent that money can be diverted because it is no longer needed in public education. Pennsylvania ranks very low among the states on per capita school expenditures. The local districts still supply somewhat more than half of all school monies.

Higher education spokesmen have made it known during the controversy that additional funds are now needed by all levels of public education. Thus they do not favor using state funds for non-public schools.

Area intermediate units

Local school districts in the state of Pennsylvania have undergone extensive reorganization in the past three years. They have been reduced from 956 to 466 operating school systems. Except for some pending appeals from school districts, the major reorganization task has been accomplished. A natural next step following reorganization is the proposed establishment of intermediate regional administrative units to replace county superintendents. The State Board of Education has proposed an intermediate unit plan that was submitted to the legislature at the last session.

Inherent in the intermediate unit proposal is the problem of determining which counties will be included in each of the 25 proposed units. This immediately poses the problem of who will make this decision. The legislature would like to see the state board perform this task, but certain groups want it done by the General Assembly. Among other things, opponents of the plan say that the entire intermediate unit idea is a power grab on the part of the state board. These same opponents claim that such a plan would undermine local control of school districts. Before final action is taken, the bill will be extensively amended.

As mentioned above, this intermediate unit controversy serves to point up the concern that some legislators have about the power of the board. One amendment, for example, provides that services to be performed by the units are to be spelled out in law rather than by regulations of the state board. This is a clear attempt to curtail board powers and illustrates the state board-legislature relationship discussed earlier. Some claim that the legislature is acting to limit the powers of the board in deference to political pressures that surround the old county system.

The Future of Education in Pennsylvania

It is our impression that education in Pennsylvania, particularly higher education, has taken great strides forward in the past few years. The formal decision-making structure for education has been strengthened and the higher education system has been placed on a more solid financial base. There is evidence to indicate that the politics of education in the state is establishing a pattern that will provide a more stable basis for decision-making, although the relationship between the legislature and the relatively new state board is not clear. In comparison with other states, the needs of both elementary-secondary and higher education in Pennsylvania are being met with a minimum of conflict and competition. It is problematical, however, whether such a relationship can continue to exist between the educational levels. Unless new sources of revenue are found, the increasing social, political, and financial problems to be faced by the schools will cause pressure to build up which will force the educational levels into open conflict.

XII. TEXAS

Texas politics is distinctive in many ways, and some familiarity with its unique characteristics is requisite to an understanding of the politics of education in Texas. The state has had a long tradition of conservatism which still prevails in most aspects of Texas state government, including the legislature. Because the state is so large, the legislature is divided into many contending groups along both geographic and political lines. The office of the Governor of Texas is one of the weakest in the nation, which promotes the power of the legislature. These and other aspects of Texas politics have influence on the politics of Texas education.

Before exploring educational politics in depth, attention will be paid to some of the present problems and issues confronting public education in Texas. The most important of these is, of course, financing the schools. Education in Texas, as in many other states, is the largest single appropriation in the state budget. In the 1966-67 biennium, 44.5% of all state outlays were used for some facet of elementary, secondary, or higher education. To even the casual observer, it becomes obvious immediately that, in the words of one state senator, the legislature is merely "a gigantic local school board." Over the last decade there has been an increase in the cost of public education in Texas by at least 300% and the end to increasing costs is certainly not in sight. A student of educational decision-making on the state level would theorize that with such large school expenditures, competition between educational levels would be inevitable. Careful examination of the politics of education in Texas suggests that such is the case although the competition is not always overt.

Another problem facing Texas education is the improvement of the quality of education. This is, of course, related to the problem of finance, but is distinct in that it recognizes that even present available resources possibly are not being used most effectively.

The termination of racial segregation has long been a problem in Texas public education. By November 1964, ten years after the *Brown* case, about one third of the state's 862 school districts with both Negro and white children had begun desegregation. It was estimated that in 1965 only about 20% of the Negro children in the state were attending school with white children. Thus the race problem is still not solved and it is constantly a matter of concern to and pressure on the people responsible for running the schools.

The role of the junior college and, more specifically, the place of vocational-technical education has also become an important question at the state level, though its full impact has not yet been felt.

The Formal Organization of Education

The government of elementary-secondary education

The formal structure of education at the state level in Texas centers upon the Texas Education Agency (TEA) and the State Board of Education. The TEA is headed by the state board, the policy-making organ of the structure. The board is composed of 21 members elected from the 21 congressional districts that existed in Texas in 1949 when it was first created. It is specifically directed to approve the educational budget of the state, execute textbook contracts and adopt any rules and regulations necessary to carry out the state educational program. A Commissioner of Education, appointed by the board and confirmed by the Senate, is the chief executive officer of the TEA. He and his staff are responsible for carrying out the board policies, making professional recommendations, preparing the budget, etc. The TEA is one of the most important state agencies, if one uses the criterion of money, for it disburses more than one-half billion dollars a year. Its own operating budget is about $3.7 million. However, the disbursement of money is not necessarily a good measure of the importance of a state agency, at least not of the importance of the TEA. Despite the large responsibility for distribution of resources, the TEA is rather ineffective in influencing state level educational policy-making.

In the opinion of some legislators and university professors, the State Board of Education is a farce. They claim that it is made up of "well intentioned but incompetent laymen who have been elected, in effect, by local teachers' groups." In fact, the teachers' groups are the only ones who do seem really interested in the board.

An observer of the educational decision-making process in Texas who looked only at the formal decision-making structure would expect to find the TEA the dominant influence in policy-making. This, however, is not the case, for there appears to be an informal structure which exerts great influence on elementary-secondary decisions in the state. The main component of that structure is the Texas State Teachers Association (TSTA) which maintains a powerful lobbying group in the state capital.

The governor's office also exerts considerable influence on decisions affecting elementary-secondary education. The extent of the governor's influence and the role of the legislature in educational decision-making is illustrated by the maneuvering used to obtain passage of a teacher's pay raise bill in the Sixtieth Legislature (1967).

It is important to note that the composition of the Texas legislature has changed in recent years in a manner which has benefited education in the state. There is increased representation from population centers such as Houston, Dallas, Fort Worth and San Antonio. The urban legislators bring to Austin a deep concern for city problems, and especially school problems. In addition to the increase in urban representation, both houses now have Republican members and both now have Negro representatives. These changes in the complexion of representation are partly responsible for the unusual success of education bills in the Sixtieth Legislature. This session will be remembered as the "Education Session"—it provided the largest amount of money ever appropriated for teacher pay raises. The $60 million in new funds appropriated for pay increases effective September 1967 brought teacher's salaries in Texas to about the national average.

The complex series of events in the legislature leading to the final passage of the pay raise bill illustrates several important aspects of educational decision-making in Texas. First, the pay raise bill did not actually originate in the legislature, but seems to have had its origin in the governor's office and the office of an interest group—the TSTA. To obtain passage of this pay raise bill, the governor used all the traditional tools of his office to influence the legislature. He included in his recommendations legislation that encompassed about one third of the program proposed by TSTA. The reason for this conservative proposal was that the governor did not wish to show favoritism to elementary-secondary education because of the possible friction such favoritism would cause among college faculty who have not fared particularly well in Texas.

The governor also used his influence with individual legislators to obtain passage of the bill. Even though the office of governor is weak, it has considerable control over the activities of the legislature and, in this case, over the fate of Texas teachers. Because of the deep involvement of the governor and his staff, the TEA chose not to become seriously involved despite the importance of the legislation at issue. There was little effort on the part of TEA officials to influence the course of events once they had been started on their way.

Budget preparation and presentation for elementary-secondary education

Requests for appropriations for financing elementary-secondary education are directed to the governor. The governor of Texas operates with a very small personal staff which includes two people who serve as the executive budget division in addition to serving as administrative assistants. This budget staff receives requests for appropriations and compiles them into a document which is submitted with recommendations to the Legislative Budget Bureau. The Legislative Budget Bureau consists of designated members of the house with a large staff which reviews agency budget requests in detail and submits a budget document to the legislature. This document traditionally has been more detailed than the governor's, and it has been the one from which the legislature operates in its appropriation process.

The government of higher education

There are twenty-two state supported senior colleges and universities in Texas. The administrative control of these institutions is vested in twelve different boards of trustees, each of which is composed of nine non-salaried members appointed by the governor for six-year terms. Included among them are the Board of Regents of the University of Texas System, the Board of Directors of the A & M College System and the Board of Regents of the State College System, the latter of which supervises seven colleges and universities.

Some time ago it was recognized that unless some order and coordination could be brought to the college and university system, there would soon be major chaos in higher education in Texas. In 1955, the Texas Commission on Higher Education (TCHE) was created to serve as a central coordinating agency for public higher education. Even though the TCHE remained in existence until 1965, it was apparent not long after its creation that it lacked adequate authority to provide the desired coordination. It was not able, for example, to prevent the addition of new four-year colleges even though the others were inadequately financed, and it was also unable to control degree programs within various institutions. It was replaced in 1965 by the Coordinating Board, Texas College and University System.

The Coordinating Board is composed of eighteen unsalaried members appointed by the governor for six-year staggered terms. The board serves as a policy-making body, with an appointed Commissioner of Higher Education to serve as its administrative officer. The Coordinating Board has such major functions as these:

1. to prescribe the role and scope of each college and university,

2. to recommend tuition policies for the various institutions,

3. to develop criteria to be used as a basis for determining the need for new institutions of higher education,

4. to control and supervise the junior colleges and to encourage and develop, in cooperation with the State Board of Voca-

tional Education, new certification programs in technical-vocational education,

5. to exercise the power of deletion and consolidation of courses taught in any institution of higher education,

6. to provide enrollment projections for use in disbursement of tax funds,

7. to devise formulas for the use of institutions in the preparation of budget requests.

The functions reserved for the Coordinating Board seem likely to have a mixed effect on the relations between educational levels. Its power to control and supervise junior colleges and to develop new certification programs in technical-vocational education could lead to competition. The power to delete and consolidate courses taught in any public institution of higher education is highly controversial. Such authority, if wrongly used, could threaten academic freedom. Furthermore, it is questionable if this power of the board is necessary for effective coordination.

It is obvious after examining the functions of the board that it is a regulatory and not an advisory board, since the board has the power to approve programs and to control budget formulas. By virtue of the fact that the board must approve funds spent for any program it is endowed with enforcement as well as regulatory powers.

Since the creation of the Coordinating Board, there has been an optimistic feeling that the future of Texas higher education will improve. Financial support has already increased and leadership has improved. For the 1966–67 biennium, about 12.4% of total state spending was appropriated for all categories of higher education. Not all persons concerned with higher education are optimistic, however. Some feel that the board's authority in the budgeting or appropriation process is less than that of the former TCHE. The extent to which the board can present a financial program for all higher education is dependent, outside of the formula, on requests by the governor and the legislature. It remains a moot question whether the legislature will permit the development of a strong coordinating body for higher education. The board does not presently appear to be in particularly good standing with the legislature. It may be that the board will always be unpopular and opposed by influential members of the legislature and the executive branch who are considered to be friends of the teachers and of education in general, for the board represents something of a threat to particular educational interests. In the legislature, it also embodies the threat of increased executive-branch influence over educational policy.

Legislators and administrative officials who do not have faith in the present set-up in higher education have suggested that the state will eventually have to create an overall coordinative body to deal with education from kindergarten through doctoral degrees.

Education in the thirteenth and fourteenth grades

Junior colleges in the state of Texas have received considerable attention in the last few years. They are recognized as a significant part of the higher education structure in the state. Since 1965 the junior colleges have been administered through the Coordinating Board for the Texas College and University System. Prior to that date they were the responsibility of the Texas Education Agency. This shift in responsibility occurred because the TEA was not devoting adequate energies to the junior college programs. In addition, it was apparent that the junior colleges had more in common with higher education than elementary-secondary education. It is still too early to determine definitely whether the shift has halted the unplanned, nondirected growth of junior colleges which usually led to power fights on the floor of the legislature. Some hope that the junior colleges will become a part of a master plan for higher education with course offerings determined by a strong central coordinating board.

There is a considerable amount of evidence to indicate that both the governor and the legislature realize that the junior colleges hold the key to the solution of many of the higher education problems in Texas. In January of 1967, the governor, in his budget message, recommended doubling junior college funds. The legislature responded to this request by providing the 36 public junior colleges with the largest percentage increase in the college appropriations bill. It is certain that such increases for junior colleges will soon be viewed by both the state colleges and the public elementary-secondary schools as a definite threat. The various educational leaders have not yet seemed willing to acknowledge this fact.

There is another dimension of junior college training that is increasing in importance, that of vocational-technical education. Although the junior colleges still emphasize academic courses, the state has become interested in promoting vocational and technical education in the thirteenth and fourteenth grades. Vocational-technical education at this level is a relatively new effort. At present, the vocational-technical function overlaps both elementary-secondary and higher education, but its structure is something of an enigma. At the present time, vocational-technical education is being administered through the TEA while the junior colleges are under the Coordinating Board. Such organization is explainable since there is vocational-technical training in the secondary schools, but the structure does not appear to be workable. It has been suggested that the TEA contract with the Coordinating Board to coordinate all vocational-technical education. Such an arrangement would serve both groups better financially as well as administratively.

Financing Education in Texas

Before the relationship between elementary-secondary and higher education financing can be fully analyzed, it is necessary to review the complicated fund structure in the state, though we cannot explore this topic in detail. The General Revenue Fund is the focus of attention by those interested in education, and it is also the fund from which the state finances its hospitals, universities, and many other services. Here is where almost all legislative action affecting the cost of government is eventually felt. It is in seeking revenue from the General Fund that competition between levels of education occurs. Both elementary-secondary and higher education turn to the General Revenue Fund when the foundation program demands are not met from other sources. Its importance is heightened by the fact that the foundation program is tied to minimum teachers' salary levels. It is for this reason that the pressure for teacher pay raises is on the legislature rather than on the local district. Since both higher education and elementary-secondary make demands on the General Revenue Fund, the governor and the legislature must consider the two levels of education, at least to some degree, within the same frame of reference.

So far there has been no overt clash over funds between the various levels of education, but some students of Texas educational politics feel the 1967 legislative session was probably the last at which a collision could be avoided. They feel that the state is reaching the limits of its resources and one important sign of this is that the Governor's Committee on Public School Education, which will report in 1968, is ready to make recommendations that will require additional tax sources. It will be the responsibility of the Governor's Committee to identify these new sources, and there is no doubt that whatever recommendations are made, they will affect the tax structure. No matter what is proposed, both higher education and elementary-secondary will require additional support. In any event, it will not be long before there will be a clash. The competition is still not overt, but teachers at all levels are always going to seek pay raises and the competition will inevitably become more keen. It can be anticipated that junior college and vocational-technical needs will also intensify this competition.

Concluding Observations

We have analyzed some of the areas of potential conflict between elementary-secondary and higher education in Texas. The future of public education in Texas seems destined for increased competition among the levels of education, and the next session of the legislature may well be the forum for this confrontation. A major reason is that two influential study groups will have made recommendations prior to the start of the 1969 session. One is the 15-member Governor's Committee on Public School Education, which is focusing on every facet of elementary-secondary education. Its final report will include long-range proposals for improving the public schools. The Coordinating Board also will issue its Master Plan for Higher Education at about the same time. Evidence of the anticipated impact of these study groups is the fact that the governor has declined to recommend a broad-based tax increase at this time, since it is his opinion that substantial new taxes will be needed in 1969 to finance the proposals of the two educational study committees.

	Comparative Analysis
3	*of Some Major Elements*
	in Interlevel Relations

Any analysis of the material presented in the preceding pages runs risks of oversimplifying a complex subject. The reader must be reminded again of the fluidity of the educational scene, the elusive nature of the problem, and the intangibility of much of the pertinent evidence. He must also keep in mind that this was intended to be an exploratory effort, and that for the most part, as we have indicated earlier, it takes account of the situation only through the summer of 1967. With these qualifications, this chapter attempts to provide some comparative comment on relations between elementary-secondary and higher education in the twelve states studied.

The opening chapter of this report made the point that in most respects the division between elementary-secondary and higher levels of education has been so firmly established as to seem entirely natural. The institutions of education, the public organizations that run them, methods, philosophies, educational careers—all tend to break between the twelfth and thirteenth years. It has become quite habitual to think of these as two distinct educational worlds. But however accustomed such thinking and action may be, its logic can be questioned. Beyond the arguments of convenience and familiarity, there appear to be few reasons for cutting education at any given point into distinct compartments, and many of the reasons that have historically been cited (for example, those based on theories of child development or economic need) are made obsolete by new perspectives or social change.

Many of these forces of social change are themselves pushing for the revision of outlooks on this phase of education as on many others. Education is, in many senses, being taken more seriously in the United States now than ever before, and it is an increasingly substantial charge on public resources. Public schooling, in tune with a complex urban society, is an ever more elaborate process, requiring better facilities and better personnel. The age distribution of the population puts an extraordinary proportion of Americans into the bracket of school clientele. Furthermore, the demands of a specialized and productive economy place emphasis on a trained, rather than a mass, labor force. Such trends have raised the price of education, making it one of the nation's biggest businesses, and they have pressed for reexamination of established practices in terms of benefits, costs, efficiency, effectiveness, and the like.

Thus have developed some of the conditions that question the traditional separation between elementary-secondary and higher education. These conditions are felt differently from place to place and from time to time, as the summary reports on various states indicate in the foregoing pages. This chapter is an effort to show how they are felt and to approach questions about why the similarities and differences are as they are.

With a subject so generalized and complex, it is difficult to find a completely satisfactory set of summary concepts with which to work. Perhaps the most obvious are the concepts of conflict and cooperation, familiar in social science but fairly consistently vague. Relationships between educational levels in the various states can be described as more or less characterized by conflict, more or less subject to cooperation. They may even be thought to fall along a continuum running from manifest conflict through latent conflict and quiescence to cooperation; in a crude way this analysis makes use of such a pattern. As a rigorous mode of analysis it is seriously flawed. The concepts themselves are ambiguous, and conflict and cooperation are probably not suitably seen as polar kinds of institutional behavior. Further, the field of interlevel relations is a multi-dimensional, multi-issue, multi-institutional sort of thing. It is not just conceivable but true that on one issue within a state interactions might be pleasant and constructive and on others bitter or cool.

Although both our subject and our data must limit our pretensions to rigor, we can, with qualifications, speak of these relationships in terms of conflict and cooperation. Reviewing the evidence before us, the general picture looks about as follows. In very few states has open political conflict or anything approaching it broken out between educational levels. In some few instances there has been friction of a fairly explicit sort, usually over some particular issue on which interests converge. At the other end of the scale, there is likewise very little that can be called cooperation of a generalized, institutionalized sort. Mechanisms for broad coordination between levels exist in only three of the study states, and these are so new that their effects on behavior and the distribution of resources can be judged only in tentative ways. At the same time there are numbers of instances of cooperation, sustained or temporary, in the handling of particular kinds of problems. Cooperation, like conflict, is usually *ad hoc*, but tendencies can be noted among the states studied.

We have been concerned with patterns of activity among institutions and groups, and in addition with outlooks, estimates, and attitudes about relations in education. Whether or not the objective interests of the two levels are in conflict, it is of great importance whether or not they are seen to be. Conscious awareness of the interlevel relationship is likely to have a bearing on the way problems are defined and stated, and on the institutional settings into which they are thrust.

Our research has not used a sophisticated instrument to probe this question. Interviews suggest, however, that in most states most of the leaders in education and government continue to think of elementary-secondary and higher levels as distinct if not unrelated spheres of action. A fair number of people volunteered comments about the potential for conflict. Few suggested that devices for coordination across levels are an immediate need, even when probed on the question. Very few saw generalized conflict between levels as a part of the current picture in educational politics. Most of the apprehension about the development of conflict in the future was expressed by people in the elementary-secondary sector, with some predictions about such possibilities coming from state policy-makers and little from higher education. Awareness of the potential of difficulty is probably highest in states where higher education has undergone the fastest recent development and where coordination of higher education has been institutionalized.

Little thought, apparently, is given to the relations between levels as a general phenomenon or problem. For specific issues the opposite is true. When questioned about present or potential issues in which both levels are interested, respondents commonly described interactions involving both conflict and cooperation and commented about probable courses of relationships in the future. In the field of finance, for example, concern about conflict was expressed by some people in states where public and higher education expenditures are drawn from quite separate sources. In a fashion typical of American politics, most of those involved see the politics of education as a batch of discrete problems that are handled one by one and interconnected only by the incidental compulsions of content. The possible consequences of this piecemeal outlook on the future of educational organization and decision-making will be discussed at a later point in the report.

The fact that relations between levels are seldom seen as a general problem, however, can by no means lead to the conclusion that they are of no importance. We have already mentioned more than once the forces that are making for greater interaction between the two levels and are likely to exert even greater pressure in the immediate future. These forces are making a problem—or perhaps better a set of problems—where there was none before, or at least none easily identified. Our concern is with the way this set of developments is manifesting itself, and with the way it relates to the other elements of the political world in the states touched by our study. Our investigation has led us to the conclusion that most states are nearing the point where either open political conflict between levels may be expected or where new (though not necessarily formal) means of coordination must be found.

The Changing Complexion of Interests in Educational Politics

Perhaps the proximate cause of change in the relationships between elementary-secondary and higher education, if not the most fundamental, is the changing pattern of power within the sphere of educational politics as a whole. While the details differ substantially from place to place, a good deal of similarity is apparent, and it seems quite clear that shifts of an important sort are now under way in most states.

Over the past few decades a common pattern has taken shape in the politics of education in many jurisdictions. Its bases have been the professionalization of the public schools and the universality of free public education. Through these trends teaching and auxiliary services have come to be regarded as esoteric—fit to be run only by people with special qualifications. The entire society has been made dependent on the activities of the people within the field. Thus teacher training and certification and specialized training for administrators and other professionals were established some time ago as gateways to employment in education. These steps promoted a sense of common bond among the practitioners, creating a basis for the development of strong professional groups, many of which united people from the variety of specialties that serve elementary and secondary schools, including the classroom teachers.

The sense of professionalism in education prompted these people and their organizations to behave according to the models supplied by other professional groups in society. They employed rhetoric that emphasized their service to the public. The creation of this image doubtless enhanced the standing of education with other elements in the society and facilitated the creation of alliances with a variety of interests. Education has thus come to be a socially recognized and respected profession with a good deal of influence over the conduct of its function.

Politically, this has meant that these forces have had a major voice in the resolution of educational problems. By sheer numbers, the classroom teachers, through their organizations, have tended to dominate the scene. They have formed firm alliances with groups of administrators and specialists and often with school board associations. The high social value placed on education and the very wide spread of educational interests through the society have enhanced the power of the profession and brought it into a close relationship with lay groups, including, but not limited to, those specifically education-oriented. In state after state an education coalition has formed, sometimes even loosely organized around a periodic conference or the like. These coalitions, built around the teachers' associations, have been critical elements in the politics of education in most states. And in most, their interests have been confined almost entirely to elementary and secondary school affairs.

Our investigations have led us toward the conclusion that changes are coming over this picture and that these changes are of great importance for the elementary-secondary and higher education relationship. In short, there are widespread indications that the traditional form of educational politics is breaking down. The causes of the shift are several. Perhaps the most obvious is the rise of teacher militancy, which has brought about deep divisions within the profession itself. In some places there are now two major organizations vying for power where before there was only one. And in other places the mere threat or example of militancy has raised the demands and depressed the "responsible" image of the teachers associations. Allied groups, either fearful for their own interests or disaffected by new teachers' attitudes, have tended to pull away.

Another contributory factor has doubtless been the increasing tendency to question established educational aims and practices. To some degree this dates from Sputnik, to some degree it is linked to the visibility of the schools in an education-conscious society, and to some degree it is an outgrowth of the tremendous amount of resources being dedicated to this function.

Whatever the reasons, it is apparent that a shuffling of forces is under way. To a greater or lesser extent this is true in all states in our sample. Settled routines and expected patterns of action are not to be relied on so much as they formerly were. While respondents in the states still describe the teachers associations as very powerful, in nearly all of them the description was qualified by comments about the changing situation. The consequence is fluidity in the politics of education, the "establishment" no longer being the rock upon which all else is founded.

The politics of higher education in the states has developed in significantly different ways and with more variation from place to place. The basis of the political power of the state universities has rested not so much on the professional educators as on alumni and in some instances on outside groups who stand in some sort of clientele relationship to the institutions. The latter, for example, notably include the farmers served by agricultural extension services. As to the former, legislatures and other offices are often filled in great part with loyal graduates of the state universities, especially in the midwest and west where public higher education has long been dominant.

Such support has usually constituted an effective, if not particularly cohesive, structure for the exertion of influence. It has been dampened somewhat by two factors, the fact that until recently the college-educated comprised only a small portion of the adult population, and the fact that in many states higher education has been divided among rival institutions. The first is obviously undergoing change, the second is being alleviated in some states by the development of coordinating structures, whose influence we will discuss below. Though the political power of the public colleges and universities is still fragmented and limited, it is generally in a period of growth and consolidation.

These changes in the climate of educational politics in the states constitute a kind of base-line for the development of new interlevel relations. They afford a broad political explanation for many of the alterations we see taking place in the definition of educational issues, the ways they are handled, and the structures involved. These will be reviewed in greater detail in the sections that follow. The substantive point of this is that the decline of the established pattern has created something of a vacuum of political direction in the field.

Structures of Educational Government

Political scientists have discovered reasons to doubt, in recent years, that the structure or form of government is a very important independent determinant of output in the political system. It may, however, exert an influence on the shape of political activity, and it probably can delay or redirect the force of social demands. In many circumstances it is probably an important intervening factor in the overall operation of systems of politics.

The structure of educational government does seem to have some importance to the development of new relationships between elementary-secondary and higher education levels. The states have organized themselves along different lines on both levels, and these differences appear to be reflected in reactions to the pressures of change. Perhaps even more consequential is the tendency, realized in some few states, toward the creation of governing or coordinating boards that reach across levels.

On the elementary-secondary level, our small sample includes states with various basic structures—indeed, there are almost as many basic structures as states. Thus we have described states with elective boards and appointive superintendents (Ohio), appointive boards and elective superintendents (California), elective superintendent and no board (Illinois), *ex officio* board with elective superintendent (Florida), both board and superintendent appointive, etc. These structures have often been built in a piecemeal way and in response to particular cultural and political pressures. Generally speaking, they seem to represent different ways of seeking some common objectives, especially the isolation of education from the broader arena of politics, the relief of legislatures and executives from educational responsibility, and the reinforcement and preservation of the influence of the profession in control of the educational system. Almost without exception these structures are clumsy, cumbersome, and lacking in administrative coordination with the rest of the state government.

With few exceptions, the state departments and boards of education have been closely linked with the organized education profession and its allies. It is not unusual in American government, of course, for agencies to be highly dependent on the political support and guidance of the private groups whose interests they regulate or promote. Indeed, this kind of relationship is quite typical. In education it is sometimes accomplished through formal requirements on the qualifications of those appointed to superintendencies or boards. More often, it is the outgrowth of less formal situations. Superintendents, whether elected or appointed, almost always come from the ranks of the profession and often are, in effect, nominated by it. They, in turn, have the equipment to assume leadership over the board —the time, staff, professional status, and expertise to undertake the agenda-making and information-supplying functions that count so heavily in governmental decision-making today.

This combination of private power and public authority has dominated educational policy in many states. The two sectors have worked together to develop a program and promote its enactment. One sector is sometimes described as the "tool" of the other, but the important thing is the interaction and the influence it has often managed to generate, especially in the legislative bodies of the states.

With the alteration and perhaps decline of the power of the professional "establishment" in some places, the role of the state structure has often grown unsettled and ambiguous. In some states the trends we have described earlier in this chapter, especially teacher militancy and public pressure on education, have put a definite strain on relationships, and occasionally these have erupted into open conflict. More usually, however, the situation is one of uneasy alliance, with each element more independent of the other than could have been the case a few years ago. The NEA affiliate teachers' associations cannot afford to be too closely identified with the official structure, and the state offices wish to avoid the embarrassment of too much contact with the newly-aggressive teachers.

The political result is disorganization and loss of initiative in decision-making for elementary-secondary education. Where settled patterns of action have begun to break down, nothing has developed to take their place. Legislatures that once knew where to look for cues on educational policy and were contented with the arrangement have lost their sources of certainty about what is educationally acceptable and politically feasible. Two tendencies may follow, either singly or in combination: a vacuum may develop and chaos or neglect overtake state educational policy; or legislatures themselves may begin to take on more of the responsibility for policy formulation. Such things are happening in some states; the difficulties many are experiencing with problems in the critical areas of school finance and teacher bargaining probably reflect the loss of political order in education. The important point for our purpose is that the familiar political defenses of elementary-secondary education are down. Here both the cumbrousness and the political isolation of the typical state structures for the government of education become pertinent again, for they partly explain the inability of these agencies to move strongly into leadership positions in policy development.

In terms both of past conditions and present trends, higher education in the states presents a quite different structural picture. Here again structures vary considerably from state to state, but typically the process has been one where a state legislature sets policy in response to the recommendations of one or several university governing boards. The private sector participants in the process were described briefly above; they have usually been neither so organized nor so influential in higher education as in elementary-secondary. For this reason the structures of authority have usually assumed proportionately more importance in the former field. At the same time, the political challenges to higher education have characteristically been lighter, and as a whole it has neither needed nor developed as much political leverage as the elementary-secondary level. Its strength has been diffused among institutions, academic and professional programs, and outside interests, with many lines of cleavage among them.

As in elementary-secondary education, these political conditions have been undergoing change. Social demands on higher education and social investments in it have risen in a dramatic way, so that it is no longer a rather peripheral zone of political concern. Probably the most consequential aspects of change in the politics of higher education have been those related to the structure of its government. While authority systems in elementary-secondary education have been declining in political influence, reforms at the higher level have made the exercise of influence there more focussed and effective.

The vehicle through which this change has occurred in some states is the coordinating agency for higher education. As yet, these exist in only a few states, and where they do exist they are often new, undeveloped and untested. Like other institutions, they also differ radically from state to state and exert different amounts of influence in different ways. Again the particulars may be consulted in the preceding chapter. In some states—for example, Ohio and increasingly California—the higher education coordinating bodies are strong with legislatures and play substantial roles in the development of policy. In others, including Texas and Pennsylvania, they are said to be less strong and have less developed policy roles.

In these circumstances it is difficult to generalize with much certainty about the impact of such bodies. However, there is some reason to believe that their presence has a tendency to raise the level of conflict between higher and elementary-secondary education. The difficulties of measuring conflict levels were mentioned above, and they certainly inhibit the drawing of conclusions here. But our estimates suggest that where higher education coordinating councils have been developed they are seen as a threat to elementary-secondary interests and in some cases have cut into the latter's traditional sphere. This is the case particularly where elementary-secondary education has lost some of its cohesion in the fashion described above. As higher education has gained focus it has moved into perhaps a portion of the favored political spot formerly occupied by the public school interests, a case of a familiar political maxim in operation. The manifestations of this shift in power will be noted subsequently in our discussion of specific issues at stake in educational policy-making. The point we wish to emphasize here is that the creation of a new formal structure has altered the distribution of political power, a consequence of coordination in higher education probably unintended and unanticipated.

Yet another structure of educational government that has some bearing on interlevel relations is the overall coordinating mechanism, the board or council charged with overseeing both elementary-secondary and higher level affairs. With the exception of the New York Board of Regents, all such institutions in our sample states are relatively new, newer than the coordinating agencies for higher education described in the last few paragraphs. For the most part their functions are confined to planning and recommending, though some have power to comment on budgets and approve or disapprove programs.

These boards represent structural responses to the main problem with which this study dealt, the problem of interlevel relations in education. They are attempts in states like Georgia and Massachusetts to impose order on the entire educational field through creation of a formal high-level connective tissue. The question is, do they accomplish this purpose?

Experience with these devices is yet thin and therefore the evidence is incomplete. It is our impression, however, that where there are overall coordinating agencies there tends to be less conflict between educational levels. This does not necessarily mean, if true, that the coordinating agency causes a reduction in conflict; it may be the case that such institutions are likely to be formed only where the climate of relationships is fairly good. Or it may be that they reduce the impression of conflict but not the fact of it, *i.e.*, that they create the feeling that problems in interlevel relationships will be solved because there is an institution to do it.

It should be noted that there are deviant cases in our sample, too. Of the states that we judge to be low in interlevel conflict, four (Georgia, Massachusetts, New York, and Pennsylvania) have some overall coordinating mechanism and one (Indiana) does not. Of the states we found medium or high in conflict two (Florida and Michigan) have them and four (California, New Jersey,

Ohio, Texas) do not. The association is strong but not perfect (though few are); we should also note that our ranking of states is relative and somewhat impressionistic.

In summary, our evidence indicates that institutional forms do have a relationship to the phenomena of interlevel conflict and cooperation in education. This relationship we have detected at three points: (1) Some of the characteristic organizational aspects of the government of elementary-secondary education, in combination with changes in its political alliances, seem to have vitiated its political cohesion and influence. (2) The development of coordinating agencies in higher education seems to have raised by some degree its capacity to make itself felt politically. (3) The creation of overall coordinating mechanisms in education appears to have had some effect in depressing interlevel conflict. One should not, however, draw the automatic conclusion that the revision or invention of formal structures by itself will necessarily affect the realities of interlevel politics. The structures themselves should be seen as dependent on more fundamental aspects of the political system, and hence as intervening influences in the total picture.

State Political Structure and the Interlevel Relationship

Despite the fact that there are substantial variations in political structure among the states, these do not seem to be linked in systematic ways to the matter of interlevel relations. It may be useful, however, to comment briefly on the roles played by various state institutions in the development of the subject.

Of those institutions that reach beyond the specific sphere of educational policy and administration, the legislature appears to be the most critical in dealing with contacts between levels. In most states, legislatures have maintained a fairly active interest in public school affairs, usually responding to a fair extent to the prodding and prompting of the official-unofficial education coalition. Both the system of finance and the actual appropriation of funds have generally been questions in whose disposition legislatures have taken initiative. In addition, they have helped in the development of that body of law that has encouraged the professionalization of the field and limited the discretion of the local school authorities. Thus they are accustomed to dealing with public school problems, often in some detail.

Governors, on the other hand, have been less active in the elementary-secondary field, perhaps because of the tradition that dictates the separation of politics and education. While governors have sometimes shown initiative in these matters, either by recommending programs or sponsoring study efforts, their participation seems less regular. We have noted before that state education agencies tend to be separated from other executive branch departments by institutional arrangements, and in many states, governors have operated on the premise that they should pretty much be allowed to go their own way. In four of the states in our sample the chief school officer is elected and politically independent of the governor; in a fifth the state board is elected. In all of the former the superintendent (or commissioner) has sometimes been a member of the opposing party from the governor in recent times. Regular participation in educational policy-making has been characteristic of the state office, state board, "education coalition," and legislature, with the governor somewhere on the periphery. In education, as in other fields, legislatures have usually developed specialist members and committees on whom much of the function of communication and leadership falls.

In higher education the picture looks somewhat different. Legislatures have not often exercised such detailed control over the colleges and universities as over elementary and secondary schools. Both the scale and the character of the two levels have distinguished them from each other. As we pointed out earlier, legislatures have not had to deal with the magnitude or type of outside pressure from higher education as from the public school interests. This is not to say that higher education has been aloof from legislative politics, but that its involvement has been less deep and less consistent.

As higher education has gained in importance, however, it has increasingly found favor with education-minded governors. Perhaps looking for ways of promoting the educational status of their states and discouraged with the ponderousness of the elementary-secondary structure, several have identified themselves with the growth of their public college and university systems. Through political support, sponsorship of planning, expansion, and coordination studies and the like, they have put their mark on higher education. This appears to have been part of the story in such states as New York, Ohio, New Jersey, and Pennsylvania.

Meanwhile, as we have already explained, with the disorganization of political power in elementary-secondary education, legislatures are put in a position of greater freedom and responsibility. In some states we were told that they are moving into a vacuum.

This combination of circumstances may bode well for interlevel coordination, but it will not necessarily do so. It does tend to pull the problems of both levels into the general institutions of state policy-making, where they may be seen in more holistic and relative ways. If true initiative in educational policymaking comes to reside in the interaction of governors and legislators, it may lose some of the parochial and piecemeal characteristics it has heretofore displayed. In the future, coordination between levels might be effected in the legislative-gubernatorial sphere itself, or it might come about through their creating overall coordinating boards and investing them with significant powers.

There are, however, massive and perhaps insurmountable obstacles to such things happening in many states. These obstacles are embedded in the structures and processes of state government today. While any set of generalizations cannot apply evenly to all cases, some problems are very widespread. In some part, the difficulties of coordination by legislative-executive interaction are inherent in the tradition of separation of powers, which puts procedural barriers in the way of cooperation between branches. The effect of these is heightened by mutual suspicions and jealousies. In many states it is rare for one political party to control the governorship and both houses of the legislature, and in the best of circumstances the parties are not very effective connecting links on policy issues. Thus there are few forces that unite the branches of government, and many that divide them.

Ordinarily, neither branch in itself is strong, coherent, and well-equipped. Governors are often discouraged from taking educational leadership by the institutional isolation of the field. Often, the governor does not have an adequate staff, and he frequently lacks effective tools for dealing with the legislative body. The legislators themselves are notoriously ill-organized and ill-staffed, underpaid, pressed for time, and submerged by a flood of work. In these circumstances it can hardly be wondered why they have difficulties developing well-articulated programs of public policy. They are compelled, in effect, to delegate initiative to private interests and particularized state agencies. Thus state policy tends to be piecemeal, *ad hoc*, slow to respond to or anticipate changing social needs. In many respects these characteristics are built into the entire American political system.

The prospects for achieving greater policy coordination between educational levels may depend, therefore, on the development of greater effectiveness in state government generally. This does not necessarily imply that institutional reform is essential. Openness and vigor on the parts of governors and legislatures might well accomplish coordination within existing frameworks, at least in many states. In some ways the climate is now propitious for such a change, for established lines of political alliance are weakened and the relative power of the two levels is probably more even than usual. Thus there is give and fluidity in the situation. Some states, for example, Massachusetts and Pennsylvania, appear to be capitalizing on circumstances to move toward an institutionalized system for coordination across levels. But in light of the difficulties of mobilizing broad political power for such educational reform, it seems more likely to be the exception than the rule.

The Critical Issues

Throughout our account, certain issues have been repeatedly mentioned as the points of policy where the interests of elementary-secondary and higher education converge and where conflict or cooperation may be expected to develop. The question we must consider here is whether there is anything in the form of the issues and the circumstances surrounding them that affect the general atmosphere of interlevel relationships.

Without doubt the most portentous issue for the long run is the matter of educational finance. The general problem of finding money for the schools is a familiar one, and it has been mentioned in a variety of places earlier in this report. We will not review the details here, but in the past the approach of most states to the support of education has kept the two levels separate and free from competition with one another. To be more specific, they have by and large drawn funds from different (or seemingly different) sources. Elementary and secondary schools have been heavily dependent on property taxes drawn from local districts. The state support they have received has sometimes come from earmarked funds, and usually (in recent years) allocated according to fixed formulas. Higher education, on the other hand, has been supported from fees and charges, from federal loans and grants, and from allocations from state general funds. Most of the competition between the two has been well hidden in this complex set of traditional arrangements.

As we have pointed out before, however, this system is under pressure. On the side of higher education the pressure comes from increased costs and growing enrollments. On the elementary-secondary side it stems from the inadequacies and inequities of present arrangements. In nearly every state one hears complaints about the insufferable burden of the local property tax, complaints that usually point in the direction of an increase in state aid. Active campaigns for property tax relief are widespread, and it is no wonder that legislators are paying heed to them, for their political possibilities are immense. It is certain that most states will have to make extensive revisions in their school support and revenue systems in the near future.

As these pressures are felt, elementary-secondary and higher education sectors will be pressed into reliance on the general state revenue supply. The luxury of apparent non-competition cannot, in other words, continue for long. Either new formulas satisfactory to both levels will have to be negotiated under state leadership, or new institutions with power and confidence will have to emerge to coordinate claims. Otherwise, conflict for the favor of legislatures and governors seems inevitable.

Little of this conflict is apparent at present, though many interviewees from various parts of public life suggested that it was imminent. Certainly no other issue is so likely to bring the broad question of interlevel relationships into the open. Probably the states most likely to avoid the abrasive effects of conflict are those now gaining experience with coordination through boards whose scope includes both levels. These do not at present wield significant fiscal power, but their involvement in planning and their mere existence as a common meeting ground for educational interests may pay off handsomely in the future.

A second major issue that sometimes vexes the relationship between elementary-secondary and higher education is the control of instruction in the 13th and 14th grades. At an earlier point we reviewed some of the reasons for difficulty over this matter. Actually, the question is not just one of control but also one of orientation and basic mission. Three patterns are in use in the states we have studied. Some have committed themselves to the community or junior college pattern, with institutions in some part locally run and financed. Some have developed 13th and 14th grades on branch campuses of the established state universities. And some have utilized a combination of the two or are still seeking some satisfactory mode of approach.

Until rather recently, most states developed 13th and 14th grade instruction in a rather haphazard and accidental way. The historical patterns thus established had substantial effects on the plans for growth formulated in the last two decades, when pressure grew more acute. With the education boom and population increase that followed World War II, the demand for college-level instruction within commuting distance of a large proportion of the potential clientele became obvious as did the need to find ways of providing it on an economical basis. Under such stimuli, the states began to realize the need for longer-run and more rational planning.

Aside from the historical reasons, it is not clear why various states developed the patterns they did, *i.e.*, no particular structural pattern is evident. The states that utilized the branch campus approach tended to be those with strong public universities, for example, Ohio and Indiana, but all such states did not rely exclusively on branch campuses. California has an old and well-established university system, and also the largest network of junior colleges in the country. New York, until recently without a public university system of appreciable scale, has utilized a combination of university campuses and community colleges.

The political importance of 13th-14th grade education is that it may serve as a trigger issue for conflict or as a lever inducing cooperation. In most of our sample states, the question of orientation and control have been, at least to some degree, a matter of contention between the elementary-secondary and higher education forces, even where traditions of development point clearly toward one kind of resolution. In California, for example, the legislation establishing coordination declared the junior colleges to be a part of the higher education system even though they were historically linked to elementary-secondary districts and had been within the purview of interests of the CTA-State Department combine. In Indiana, where the branch campus device is quite firmly established, the public school groups have not been entirely happy or quiescent about the arrangement.

The junior and community college interests themselves have rarely developed a firm independent base of political power. The basic reason is that they have been split between those with the background and orientation of public school people and those who take the academic world of the college and university as their major reference group. Similarly, they are split at the policy level between forces for local autonomy and forces for central control. Interestingly enough, the junior-community college idea has great intrinsic political appeal for reasons that are rather obvious. These institutions provide education for the "masses" and put home towns on the educational map. They are an economical way of solving the public thirst for opportunity. Thus community colleges, with their wide constituencies and common-sense, practical tone are often said to be very popular with legislatures. The point, however, is that they often enjoy this favor without any coherent policy direction to it, given the schisms, competitions, and lack of settled traditions in the field.

Coordination across levels would perhaps provide some institutional corrective to the conflict generated over this issue, though it must be said that we have little evidence of the past efficacy of such structural efforts. It may well be that the key to their success would lie in creation of a strong coordinating mechanism reinforced by a strong legislative policy directive. In these circumstances the community-junior college movement might be expected to develop a sense of identity and efficacy that would permit it to act as an independent force within the broad ambit of a coherent educational politics.

Closely related to the issues discussed in these last few paragraphs is the issue of vocational-technical education. This is probably the most ambiguous of the policy areas we have encountered. In a poverty-conscious society, and one undergoing rapid technological change, the importance of education directed to fulfilling vocational and technical needs would seem to be obvious. It appears, however, that in most states the field suffers lack of direction, lack of commitment, underemphasis, and general confusion. Perhaps in this portion of education the problem is less conflict over an issue than the absence of issue substance around which conflict might revolve.

Perhaps the most characteristic state-level focus for vocational-technical education is a bureau in the state education agency. Programs tend to include some pre-graduation high school vocational work and some continuation courses under the aegis of local secondary districts. Community colleges and, more rarely, state colleges, variously offer some technical programs designed to prepare students for sub-professional types of jobs. Under federal grant legislation most states are also in process of establishing area vocational schools, usually in regional districts under state department auspices.

Only rarely does vocational and technical education seem to have occasioned conflict between educational levels. Higher education, generally speaking, has had little interest in it; even the junior and community colleges have been pushed hard by some elements toward an "academic" kind of program. Elementary-secondary education, too, has been dominated by those with orientations other than vocational preparation. Much of the effort that has been made in the vocational-technical field has been the result of the inducement powers of federal money. Some people in the states attribute the disorganization of vocational-technical education to the bureaucratic presence of the national government in the field, but we have no evidence that this charge is fair.

On the whole, vocational-technical education does not appear likely to stimulate conflict between levels of education. The problem, as we suggested before, is more that nobody cares, therefore, nobody wants it, therefore, the function goes uncoordinated and largely unfulfilled. Perhaps here, too, an organizational response like the development of a special department might stimulate the development of interest. Where that has been tried, as in Indiana, it has been the subject of some controversy and as yet not produced startling results.

Issues other than the three discussed above are much less consistently involved in the interlevel relationship. Teacher education and certification, obviously of interest to both K–12 and higher education, only occasionally appears to generate conflict. It has, in fact, served as a vehicle in a few states for the development of interlevel rapport, for example, in Indiana and New York. In California, elementary-secondary and higher education were to some extent on opposite sides of a controversy over teacher education, but the role of the colleges and universities was mixed and somewhat covert. Program articulation between secondary schools and colleges, college admissions standards, and the like were also mentioned as points of contact between levels, but without showing particular patterns or clear implications.

Environment and the Interlevel Relationship

As we pointed out in the introductory chapter, there has been a good deal of interest lately in the relationship of socioeconomic environment and political structures to the responses and activities of states and local communities. As we also mentioned there, we are severely handicapped by our small sample size in exploring these questions with reference to interlevel conflict. The question is simple enough: what factors in the social, economic, cultural, and political setting seem to have a bearing on patterns of relationship between educational levels? At best we could do no more than indicate what lines of analysis might be fruitful.

A very preliminary attempt to find some orderly answer to the question has yielded us virtually nothing. The table on pages 185–6 reports data on how states rank on a few selected contextual variables. It should be noted that the weakest variable of the lot is the most critical, interlevel conflict, the dependent term. We have no suitable quantifiable indicator and must be satisfied with a rather subjective comparative evaluation. In fact, we have simply divided the states into two groups, one higher and one lower in conflict according to our best judgment in light of all the evidence we have. The independent items include a fairly standard array, with a few on socio-economic characteristics, a few on educational expenditures, and two measures of party politics. All but the first and last items are reported on the table by rank order within the sample.

This little test gives us no reason to believe that conflict between levels varies according to such things as wealth, schooling, or urbanization of population. A very weak positive relationship shows up when conflict is measured against expenditures for elementary-secondary schooling, both as a proportion of personal income and on a per-pupil basis. That is, the higher the expenditure, the higher the level of conflict. There is far less sufficient evidence here upon which to base a conclusion, however.

A fairly substantial-looking relationship, in this case negative, does show up between party competitiveness and conflict. That is to say, inspection of the data suggests that where interparty competition tends to be higher, conflict between educational levels tends to be lower. If further evidence bore this relationship out, perhaps it might be explained as the effect of efforts to isolate education from politics in states where interparty tension threatens the independence of the schools. Such isolation may be the consequence either of setting the two levels into separate institutional frameworks that reduce their

Socio-Economic, Educational, and Party Characteristics of States by Rank Order Within Sample

	California	Florida	Michigan	New Jersey	Ohio	Texas	Georgia	Illinois	Indiana	Massachusetts	New York	Pennsylvania
Interlevel Conflict (Higher-Lower)	H	H	H	H	H	H	L	L	L	L	L	L
Population Estimated populations, 1966, from *Statistical Abstract of the United States* (Washington, D.C.: U.S. Government Printing Office, 1967), p. 25.	1	9	7	8	6	5	12	4	11	10	2	3
Median School Years Completed Median school years completed by persons 25 years old and older, 1960 Census. Office of Education, *Digest of Educational Statistics: 1967* (Washington, D.C.: U.S. Government Printing Office, 1967), p. 61.	1	3	5	8	3	10	12	9	5	2	7	11
Personal Income Per Capita Personal income per capita, 1964. U.S. Department of Commerce, Office of Business Economics, *Survey of Current Business*, 45 (July, 1965), p. 11.	2	10	6	4	7	11	12	3	9	5	1	8
Urbanism Proportion of state's population living in places with population of 2,500 or more, 1964. Research Division, National Education Association, *Rankings of the States, 1966,* Research Report 1966-R 1 (Washington, D.C.: National Education Association, 1966), p. 13.	2	7	8	1	9	6	12	5	11	4	3	10
Per Capita Expenditures—All Education Per capita state expenditures for all education, 1964. Ibid., p. 48.	1	7	2	11	10	6	5	9	4	12	3	8
Elementary-Secondary Expenditures as Percent of Personal Income Total current expenditures for public elementary and secondary schools for 1964–65 as percent of personal income in 1964. Ibid., p. 51.	1	8	1	7	6	3	5	10	10	12	3	9

Socio-Economic, Educational, and Party Characteristics
of States by Rank Order Within Sample (continued)

	California	Florida	Michigan	New Jersey	Ohio	Texas	Georgia	Illinois	Indiana	Massachusetts	New York	Pennsylvania
Per-Pupil Expenditure (A. D. A.) Per-pupil expenditure on A. D. A. basis, 1966–67. Office of Education, *op. cit.*	3	6	4	2	10	11	12	5	8	7	1	9
Party Competition The measure of party competition was calculated by averaging party votes for governors and legislators by state. Based on Richard E. Dawson and James A. Robinson, "Inter-Party Competition, Economic Variables, and Welfare Policies in the American States," *Journal of Politics*, XXV (May, 1963), pp. 265–89, esp. pp. 275–76. States are ranked 1–12 from higher to lower competition.	4	10	7	9	7	11	12	2	6	1	5	3
Party Control SD = strong Democratic, MD = moderate Democratic, DIV. = divided, MR = moderate Republican. Adapted from Thomas Dye, *Politics, Economics, and the Public* (Chicago: Rand-McNally, 1967), p. 54.	MD	SD	DIV.	DIV.	MR	SD	SD	DIV.	MR	MD	MR	MR

interactions or by creating non-political frameworks to contain and thus reduce interlevel conflict.

Otherwise, our examination yields us little in the way of indication about the contextual conditions of conflict between elementary-secondary and higher education. This fact in itself suggests that it is probably out of differences in educational history, traditions, and institutional arrangements that different patterns of interaction have grown.

Conclusion | *Trends and Directions in Educational Policy-Making*

The purposes of this study have been to describe and analyze the present relationship between elementary-secondary and higher education in selected states, and to examine the varying effects of this relationship on political processes and educational policies. Building on the evidence presented in the preceding two chapters, this chapter evaluates the current situation and reflects on trends and directions that seem probable in the future.

It should be understood that the implications of our findings may be read differently by different people. Notions about the proper shape of the political order and about the ends to be sought through educational policy may dictate various attitudes about the phenomena we have described. Some may regard coordination as an end in itself, and some may think the piecemeal quality of state decision-making as intrinsically meritorious.

The authors of this study have tried to hold themselves free from such prior commitments, but have endeavored to ask questions about what will conduce best to the health of the educational function at all levels. We are not committed to a conflict-free politics, but rather to whatever arrangements will promote both a responsive decision-making system *along with* an active concern for the overall future of education.

On the whole, we have been pushed toward the conclusion that interlevel coordination in education is a desirable, if not essential, step. Such coordination need not be and indeed would not be likely to be tight and neat. But without some effort to bring the forces of education together into some form of integrated structure, the ability of the states to undertake rational planning in education is bound to suffer. One or more of several consequences is likely to ensue. Legislatures will be asked to make policy with inadequate information and recommendatory support. Resources will be allocated without consideration of the whole range of relative needs. And some program areas, including education in 13th and 14th grades and vocational-technical training, will either lie untended in the interstices between levels or be the subject of irrelevant political bickering. In short, political decision-makers need help if they are to see the whole educational picture as their field of action.

Perhaps the two most general findings of this study seem contradictory, but actually they are complementary and point in the direction suggested above. One is that in most states the interlevel relationship verges on open political conflict. The other is that state policy-makers seldom recognize the relationship as something worthy of attention. They have been content, in the general style of American politics, to take problems piece-by-piece, confronting them only when necessary and then in as small portions as possible. The point, however, is that as the pressures rise and conflict grows, the probability of problems being handled successfully on this basis declines. The financial crisis of American education requires massive, broad scale consideration. The needs of the urban condition require quick, flexible, and insightful renovation of vocational-technical programs. More and better teachers must be recruited, trained, and effectively utilized through cross-level efforts. These and other goals seem unlikely to be reached, or at least reached in time, through bit-by-bit policy revision.

It may have been noted that we have not devoted much explicit attention to urban problems during the course of our exploration. This is the product neither of oversight nor of under-evaluation, for we agree that the most interesting and pressing of the challenges that confront American education are those of the cities. It does not appear, however, that the distinction between urban and non-urban has any particular bearing on the relationship between educational levels. In a major sense, everything we have examined is an aspect of the problems of educational policy and organization in an urban society; thus "urban" did not seem an essentially separate category of problems to be discussed. The changes that are putting pressures on established institutions are the pressures of social change, for which urbanization is a suitable short-hand expression. Perhaps this is an appropriate place to suggest that if the state-local axis in educational decision-making does not measure up to the challenges of the future, it seems likely that more power will pass to the control of the national government.

In summary, the relationship between elementary-secondary and higher education is such that it demands a united, well coordinated interlevel effort to minimize its own internal conflict and at the same time to insure its rightful share of scarce state resources. This study has not shown that educational leaders are yet capable of offering such leadership. It is clear, however, that such has to be the direction for the future.

Perhaps the heart of the relationship between elementary-secondary and higher education is the development of issues which force the problems of the two levels into a common framework of political consideration. Short of such development, they are certainly likely to go their separate ways, handled by state decision-makers piecemeal and in separate frames of reference. The issues most likely to generate a significant relationship between them at present are fiscal needs and policies on the orientation and control of 13th and 14th grades. These problems are deferrable for a time, but whether they can be deferred indefinitely in most states seems doubtful.

Once a relationship does begin to appear, its course depends on the condition of the institutions of power and authority in the state. Most often, we have found the formerly strong and cohesive forces of elementary-secondary education in situations of declining strength, and the forces of higher education not highly cohesive but on the rise. The former often lack leadership and a sense of thrust and confidence, and many of their former lines of alliance in government are less effective than before. These appear to be the circumstances in which conflict between the levels can grow, perhaps circumstances in which the equalization of power is developing.

As mentioned earlier in this chapter, the best prospect for turning the interlevel relationship away from conflict and toward cooperation, if that seems desirable, would seem to lie in the creation of new overall coordinating mechanisms. This course is neither easy nor fool-proof. It appears, however, that both the public and the private institutions of education are so rigidly separated by tradition that some "natural" accommodation is unlikely. It also seems unlikely that legislators and governors will be able to accomplish coordination without help from other agencies, unless the structures of state government are overhauled in dramatic and deep-reaching ways. They would need more time, more staff, more information, and more effective linkages among themselves to handle the broad problems of education in something better than the short-run incremental fashion in which they must now deal with most of the things they do. Perhaps in any case these steps toward revision of state structure and policy, particularly basic revenue policy, are requisite to an effective educational future.